AF352528

ALTERNATIVE AMERICAN SCHOOLS

ALTERNATIVE AMERICAN SCHOOLS

Ideals in Action

CLAIRE V. KORN

STATE UNIVERSITY OF NEW YORK PRESS

Published by
State University of New York Press, Albany

For information, address State University of New York
Press, State University Plaza, Albany, N.Y., 12246

Library of Congress Cataloging in Publication Data

Korn, Claire, V., 1933-
     Alternative American schools : ideals in action / Claire V. Korn.
        p.   cm.
     "A Japanese language version, titled Furee sukuru: sono-genjtan-to-
yume (Free schools: reality and dream), was published in Tokyo in
1984"—P. 5.
     Includes bibliographical references.
     ISBN 0-7914-0471-4 (alk. paper). — ISBN 0-7914-0472-2 (pbk. :
alk. paper)
     1. Free schools—United States. I. Title.
LB1029.F7K58   1990
371'.04—dc20   90-32304
                                                                      CIP

10 9 8 7 6 5 4 3 2 1

CONTENTS

*To my husband
whose quiet wisdom and encouragement
have let me be more*

Chapter 1

EXPLANATIONS AND AN INTRODUCTION

In 1872 the Fundamental Code of Education resoundingly proclaimed, "There shall, in the future, be no community with an illiterate family, nor a family with an illiterate person." Today this utopian goal is within sight, not in the United States of course, but in the nation which stated it, our competitor, Japan (Anderson 1975, 21).

American education has similar aims, but with one in five of our adults functionally illiterate, our ideals and our reality are separated by a gaping chasm. Although many who cannot read and write are able to perform marvelous feats, including putting on convincing acts of reading their children's report cards or their supervisor's notes, their failings exact enormous personal and societal tolls (St. John and Harman 1979).

Front page headlines are hard to ignore; "U.S. Pupils Lag from Grade 1, Study Finds" trumpeted the June 17, 1984, *New York Times*. We are told that Japanese children turn in superior test performances, especially in all-important science and math, and we put two and two together. Many educational reformers say our schools should be more like theirs. Their longer school day and year, the compulsory, standardized curriculum, the constant testing, the rigid codes of behavior—all claim their advocates. Now some of our public school students are wearing Japanese-style school uniforms.

Meanwhile, our model of educational efficiency worries and yearns

1

for reform. Some Japanese are looking for guidance from what many Americans may think an improbable source, from American alternative, open education. Schools where children "learn without compulsion" (the phrase is Japanese) are, for some, a desired utopia. They call them "free" schools, these learning environments which are continually re-created in flexible response to the ever-changing needs of children.

We Americans have a history of tolerating and occasionally encouraging visionaries who strive to create schools where children ask new questions instead of memorizing answers to the old. The teachers in these schools insist that knowledge and experience are interconnected and that learning is both continuous and social. In these schools children learn to live together and to assume responsibility for themselves and their society. From 1896 to 1903 the Chairman of the University of Chicago's Department of Philosophy, Psychology, and Pedagogy, John Dewey, and his wife directed a laboratory school where Dewey's progressive beliefs were put into practice. Influenced by Dewey, in 1914 Caroline Pratt opened a school with a goal of fostering, not dulling, children's natural desire to learn; in 1989 Miss Pratt's City and Country School celebrated its 75th birthday. Since 1925 the parent cooperative Peninsula School in Menlo Park, California, in accordance with Dewey's philosophy, has been working at matching its educational experiences with the needs of children.

Another educational experiment, Mrs. Marrietta Johnson's Organic School in Fairhope, Alabama, has followed the tenets of Jean Jacques Rousseau for more than eighty years. Rousseau insisted that education must be based on the needs and innate capacities of children, not the demands and accomplishments of adults (Dewey and Dewey 1915).

The upheavals in American society from the late 1960s to the mid-1970s, through the heated times of the Vietnam war and the Civil Rights Movement, stirred antagonism towards authority and stimulated the growth of non-traditional schools. At first small private schools sprang up, nurtured by social unrest and distrust of existing institutions. During the 1970s, public school systems got on the alternative bandwagon and developed different styles of schools. In some school districts parents and students were able to select their educational experiences from menus of alternatives. (The notion of allowing students and parents to select a school instead of being assigned by the system is attracting many adherents in 1990; advocates feel that choice and a sense of belonging will strengthen "good" schools and drive out the "bad." Opponents fear that the most needy children would be hurt by being left behind.) Among other alternatives, there were the Freedom Schools which grew out of the Civil Rights Movement and the free schools which advocated A. S. Neill-style anti-authoritarian freedom. Open classrooms practiced the methods of British informal education. The philosophical sources of these alternative schools have venerable histories influenced by Pestalozzi, Rousseau, Froebel, Tolstoi, Montessori, Dewey, Neill, and others.

In 1919, John Dewey accepted an invitation to lecture at Tokyo University—although he refused the Emperor's offer of The Order of the Rising Son. By all outward appearances Dewey's words and actions have been long forgotten in Japan, but the record breaking sale of more than six million copies of a small book written by a television personality, Tetsuko Kuroyanagi, suggests the longing for progressive, humane education still survives. When Kuroyanagi was only six years old, she, Totto-chan, was expelled from public school, a victim of her curiosity and non-conforming behavior. In *Totto-Chan: the Little Girl at the Window* she wrote that her failure had taken her to a remarkable "free" school which somehow managed to survive in the heart of Tokyo through the authoritarian and repressive days of World War II. At Tomoe School she and her classmates were given reassurance and responsibility instead of tests; they followed their own interests and learned from experience instead of omnipotent textbooks and teachers. Our bombers destroyed the school, but its influence lives on (Kuroyanagi 1981).

Alternative American Schools: Ideals in Action was written originally for the Japanese parents and educators who are worried about the monolithic authoritarianism of their nation's educational system. A Japanese language version, titled *Furee Sukuru: Sono-Genjtan-to-Yume (Free Schools: Reality and Dream)*, was published in Tokyo in 1984.

Many teachers complain that American parents have abdicated responsibility for schooling in general and homework in particular. Most Japanese parents, on the other hand, are caught up in education mania. The "education mama" throws herself headlong into every level of her children's schooling, especially that of her sons. Her task is formidable. To score well on high school and college entrance exams, all students must master a detailed curriculum mandated by the nation's central Ministry of Education. These competitive examinations alone determine a student's lifelong options. The few students who get into Tokyo University are guaranteed success; in 1975 a third of the presidents of the top Japanese companies and sixteen of the eighteen top bureaucrats in the Ministry of Education were Tokyo graduates (Rohlen 1983). Those who fail to get into a "good" college must assume lower stations in life.

The lower the test score, the lower the status. These tests take precedence over everything. Few children help with household chores; they study. Boys do not hold part time jobs or deliver newspapers; they study.

Japanese children are promoted automatically no matter how well or poorly they master their annual piece of the uniform curriculum; exclusion from the group would be shameful. Missed material simply is not repeated. Japanese journalists call this system 7-5-3 education; only 70 percent of primary school children, 50 percent of junior high students, and 30 percent of high school students are able to keep up with the frantic rate of instruction with the remainder being the "left-behinds" (Hori 1982).

It is not surprising, therefore, that educational cramming has become a multi-billion dollar Japanese industry (Lohr 1984). One out of four elementary school students and one out of two junior high students go to cram schools after their long school day (Hechinger 1986). To gain the ultimate competitive edge some parents pay up to $1,000 a week for prekindergarten summer schools in which their three- and four-year-olds are drilled up to eight hours a day, six days a week (Traeger 1984).

Recently our Educational Testing Service acknowledged that training can improve our students' college entrance S.A.T. (Scholastic Aptitude Test) scores. Our three- and four-year-olds soon may be required to go to public schools. What do we have to learn from our Japanese economic competitors?

The litany of documentable concerns about Japanese education includes adolescent suicide, school phobia, the violence and delinquency particularly prevalent in the pressure cooker junior high schools, weak backs, inability to play, everything, in fact, except achievement test scores.

Many Japanese fear their superior test scores are bought at the expense of intellectual creativity. They worry that the United States, with only twice as many people, has won thirty times more Nobel prizes in the sciences (Lohr 1984). Some maverick business enterprises are turning to their societal failures for creativity. The video game manufacturer, Namco, hires reformed juvenile delinquents and C students, one of whom, Toru Iwatani, created Pac Man (Lohr 1983).

Risk taking is dangerous in a society in which the motto, "If the nail sticks up, pound it in," is practiced in businesses and schools. It is stunning that eight Japanese children set off for Leiston, England, in 1983 to attend Summerhill, the radical free school founded by A.S. Neill. In the United States Neill's concept of educational freedom stirs little enthusiasm, but in educationally totalitarian Japan fifteen of Neill's books are in print and the Neill Society holds regular meetings (Hori 1982).

Their attraction to "free" schools was further fueled by a journalist from the *Hokkaido Shimbun Press*. On assignment in the United States in 1981, Yasushi Ohnuma sent his newspaper reports about John Holt's home schooling movement, the Parkway Program, Clonlara School, and other educational exotica. A book of his collected articles, recently in third printing, focused the public's attention on a range of possibilities of education "without compulsion." On a 1982 lecture tour Clonlara's director, Pat Montgomery, stirred her Japanese listeners with passionate accounts of her educational experiences; her lectures in turn became another book assembled by Mr. Ohnuma, and the movement began to pick up speed.

In April, 1983, a mother and her twelve-year-old son left their home and family in Nara City, Japan, to move to Ann Arbor, Michigan. Their sole reason was to allow the boy to attend Clonlara, a small, private free school based on Neill's philosophy, a school possibly more familiar to Japanese parents than Ann Arborites. In 1988 the boy graduated from Ann Arbor's public alternative Community High School.

Under present conditions these traveling young people are unable to return to Japanese mainstream education. Even the thousands of children attending traditional schools abroad find reassimilation extremely difficult. The lure of "free," open education must be extremely powerful to entice families to sever ties with all that's familiar.

My fascination with the rich possibilities of alternative, open education grew slowly. Realizations accumulated over the ten years I worked with a group of psychologists in private practice and tried to help children in emotional pain. While other psychologists consulted with the parents, with the child's and parents' permission I routinely made contact with the child's teachers and school. One revelation was that changing the school environment could help a child faster and more effectively than traditional psychotherapeutic intervention alone.

During the process of earning a Ph.D. in Counseling and Guidance from Stanford University's School of Education to add to my M.A. in Child Clinical Psychology, I read the damning indictments of our ossified schools and the optimistic reports of new educational experiments sprouting everywhere. Later, during a short tenure as a school psychologist, I had the awful realization that most children in this particular school would be helped most if the principal could be counseled into some other profession. Still later, during a six month stay in London, our ten-year-old son was able to attend a state-supported "informal" junior school, one of those schools everyone had been talking and writing about, where rabbits were on loan from the head mistress's office and the most important school rule was that children were not to retrieve balls by climbing the drainpipes to the three-story high Victorian-era roof. Finally, between jobs and full of ideas, I opened a small, private middle school, one you will meet on these pages.

When I had to leave my school for Michigan, I became involved in Community High School as a parent and volunteer, then gradually in the other schools and programs described on these pages. This book came about because, adrift in a new community, I found Clonlara School in the Yellow Pages and dropped by to see what was going on. I have accompanied Japanese teachers and television crews to these schools where I have been an observer, participant, parent, volunteer, and even paid professional. I have tracked small children on their journeys to adulthood. I have followed published research and had access to files of test data and to unpublished evaluations of educational outcomes.

These particular innovative schools were selected because they: a) differ in organizational style but are similar in basic goals; b) were accessible and would tolerate me as a visitor; c) represent both public and private learning environments; and d) describe education for children from preschool through high school. Together the schools form a representative, although far from exhaustive, sample.

Similarly the research cited in answer to questions about alternative, open education is not exhaustive, but, overall, representative of the general findings. Easily executed, well-controlled experimental designs and open or "free" education tend to have antithetical philosophical foundations. The imaginative and time-consuming Eight-Year Study and the High/Scope research are significant exceptions.

I have tried to impart the atmosphere and flavor of these learning environments along with their philosophical foundations, their problems, and their potential. Although Japanese interest and concern were the impetus for this book, its contents may challenge Americans to think about our own schools.

Publisher Daikichi Suzuki, founder of the Japanese Free School Study Association, says, "We won't copy your American free schools, but we can learn many things from you as we borrow your strength to change our education." Often we fail to value our own strengths, including our diversity and flexibility. Since the mid-70s Community School District 4 in East Harlem has been practicing the ideal of allowing parents to select the style of public school to best meet their children's needs. Now "schools of choice" are being presented as a real alternative to the traditional concept of neighborhood schools. Instead of searching for the one, single, all-encompassing "right" way to educate our children, we might learn from exploring these successful byways, by traveling off the beaten educational track.

Chapter 2

ONE TEACHER'S DAY

A visitor can learn most of what there is to know in a short visit to a traditional school, but understanding the rhythms, the expectations, and accomplishments in one of our innovative schools is a long, slow process. Activities are self-directed and interactive, not commanded and completed. Success and failure have more to do with individual goals than test scores. At any given moment several students may seem to be playing and/or socializing while others are deeply involved in different academic-appearing activities. If a teacher is neither setting group tasks nor giving group explanations, if a teacher is neither collecting papers nor assigning grades, just what does he or she do all day?

Joan Goldsmith told me she usually gets to school by eight, but I can't find her anywhere when I arrive to spend the day watching her in action. Assured that time usually is a flexible commodity in this school called "open," I'm a few minutes late. Joan has been in and out of several rooms by the time I catch up with her.

8:15—Wearing low-heeled shoes and clutching a handful of dittoed papers, a woman with short white hair and intense blue eyes scurries down the school corridor. "It's busy work, math mania," the teacher explains with a wry look. "I hate it, but sometimes it has its uses." Joan Goldsmith goes on to say that since Halloween and Election Day many of her kindergarten through third graders have been in a wild state and she had had to tighten up to survive. Now some had gotten interested in worksheets. "This isn't

9

a typical day," she says, "but then I don't know what is."

We reach the double room she shares with a longtime colleague and friend. A playhouse area stocked with dress-up clothes, dolls, and some child-size furniture bridges the permanently open folding door. A ten-year-old sized boy comes in while she puts the worksheets in a stack of boxes towering over her buried desk top. "Are you going to visit today, Jake?" she asks and he says he wants to. "Take the chairs off the desks. But remember to tell Mrs. Williams where you are so she won't worry." In ones and twos bundled-up children hang up their coats, then chat, explore the room, or settle with something to do. A boy pulls a chair up to a row of aquariums and cages and feeds a hamster carrot tops.

Mrs. Bradley and her student teacher talk about the day ahead. "We have chorus at 10," is written on the board.

"Good morning, Sara my love," she greets a girl dressed in color-coordinated skirt, sweater, and knee socks, then adds, "Tell me, did you leave that mess in the corner yesterday?" Sara smiles a guilty smile. Mrs. Bradley puts her hand on the girl's shoulder and says, "You're all dressed up. Are you doing something special today?" Sara smooths her skirt and tells her teacher something I can't hear before starting to clean up yesterday's mess. I think of other ways this problem might have been handled: accusations, guilt trips, perhaps personal blame. Sara strikes me as someone usually in the center of the action.

Mrs. Goldsmith unobtrusively welcomes children while she moves around the room picking up and straightening and placing materials "they haven't seen for a while"—games, paper, blocks, etc.—on the group tables. This morning's only kindergarten student (seven more replace him in the afternoon) whispers something and she bends far down to hear his soft words. (Overhearing all the children's parts of conversations is going to be impossible, I realize. This record of a day-in-the-life-of-an-open-school-teacher is going to be full of holes.) He dumps the colored blocks she gives him on a table and with no obvious direction, begins to sort them by shape.

Two boys from another room ask for work, and while she unzips a class member's jacket the three talk seriously about what needs to be done. The boys leave with a time to return. Mrs. Goldsmith continues to put out materials. The school day hasn't formally started yet.

8:30—"Kids, we're going to have a meeting in about five minutes. Whatever you start you can go back to," the teacher announces.

Piano sounds escalate. "The rule is one at a time on the piano," Mrs. Goldsmith admonishes, and two of the three children stop pounding. She leafs through one of many books piled on a shelf next to the window, then disappears into the adjacent room. I can't follow her everywhere without standing out like a sore thumb and wonder how many times she'll dart out of sight today.

8:35—"Everybody to the rug," she announces and nineteen talking children pile into heaps on the floor. "Make a circle so no one is in front of anyone else. Do you remember how to do it?" The children shift around. "Who's missing?" the teacher asks and sits down, a link in the circle on the rug. "Yesterday it seemed as if some of the new people got bogged down in writing," she starts By parent request, this is the third year some of the children have been in her class. She asks a boy to close the book he is reading during group meeting. The teacher has just suggested that stories can start with wishes when a disembodied public address system voice fills the room. The children cheer the announced winners of the school's student council election.

(Like most of the others we will see, this school has no bells to tell students and teachers when to change activities, but I was surprised by the intrusive P.A. system. The children weren't bothered, however.)

"Think about a wish for yourself and a wish for someone else," Mrs. Goldsmith starts again. In the subsequent clamor she says, "The rule is you don't talk unless it's your turn." Most of the children follow her example and concentrate on each child as he or she relates wishes and hopes.

"I wish I could stay at home and didn't have to come to school," the kindergartner says happily. Later Joan tells me that this little boy's home life is so creative and interesting that it's hard for school to compete. When the wishes slow down, Mrs. Goldsmith says, "I wish I could fly. I've always wished I could fly. My wish for other people is peace." A few more children share before she says, "You don't have to write a story about your wishes. If you have other ideas, use them."

Four numbers are written in columns on the board under the headings, "Read, Write, Choice, Math." Usually the children decide the order of their activities although occasionally Joan will assign one to a group. "It will be hard to get all your groups in today," Mrs. Goldsmith says. "If you need math, it's in the . . . ," and she gives some general directions before children move off to different areas. She hands paper to a boy, finds a form for a math group, and gets a latecomer started. The children don't seem to notice when she leaves the room again.

She comes back with four bottles of food coloring and announces that one of today's choices is experiments with color. "The test tubes are all set up," she says. She asks what blue and red make and listens to wild guesses from the cluster of children. "Try it out," she says. Excited voices say they want to make black, to make green, brown, purple. "Don't waste the food coloring. Now if I leave your group, can you get along without fighting?"

9:15—As she floats around the room, she shows one child's homemade book to another, then she and a newly arrived parent volunteer discuss the resources they've uncovered for a class project on Iceland.

(My sense of time is awry. When I think ten minutes have passed, my watch tells me it's been only two and the classroom clock agrees. Things are happening fast here.)

9:25—"Okay boys and girls. This group should end in the next few minutes," Mrs. Goldsmith says, but the sound level is unchanged. The mother assembles a flute and, with Joan on the piano, they play a spontaneous duet. Several children stop to listen, but more ignore them.

"Group Two, take out what you're going to do." She stops a second-grader to explain that the kindergartner needs someone to play with. "Sure," he says, looking pleased, and the two go to a corner where paper and paints have been set out.

She settles briefly near different children who seem to be at loose ends. "I'm so glad you got that notebook out again," she tells a boy who has taken out his writing for the first time since Halloween. A changing retinue of two or three children follow their teacher to ask for spelled-out words, materials, or attention.

9:35—Students return from their recorder lesson and, without directions, pick up their Group Two activities.

"Can I help you, David?" the teacher asks the painters who are watching her from a distance. She holds a wet painting and says, "I remember you like orange a lot." The boys return to painting.

Twice she has talked with a passive girl sitting alone at a group table. Now she stops a boy who has picked up a math game and says, "Karen doesn't know how to play yet, but you could teach her." I expected him to turn her down cold, but instead he seems to think it's a good idea, sits next to the girl, and soon they're deep in conversation. It's the first time that Karen has seemed interested in something.

In front of the coat hooks and cubbyholes four boys have built an elaborate block maze in which the carrot-fed hamster is running from opening to opening. "I'm scared to death you're going to lose Twinkles," Mrs. Goldsmith observes, then adds, "You know, I don't see anything vaguely mathematical in what you're doing." Without a word one boy gets up and studies the materials on the math table.

Piano noises get louder but stop when Joan Goldsmith turns. She looks away and Sara thumps loud, discordant chords. "You're trying to get me mad," the teacher says. "Is your story going to be ready for reading? Can I see it?" Sara leaves the piano.

"Chorus, they've changed the time," she announces, but a small girl insists she's not going. "Aren't you preparing for a concert?" Mrs. Goldsmith asks but the child is adamant. The student teacher talks with her and she leaves.

Now she straightforwardly asks the boys with the maze to put the hamster away, then stores the colored blocks from the now vacated math table. When one of the artists asks her to look at his work, the teacher asks if he's tired of painting. As if released from a wall-less prison, he springs away to join the group mixing food coloring in test tubes. I didn't realize he wanted to stop, but his teacher did. Again she informs the block-maze builders that they have just a few minutes until clean-up. The student teacher reminds her that she's supervising recess today.

I wonder what a "traditional" teacher would think of the last formless, flowing hour and a half. I can't tell what's been accomplished. More than once Joan Goldsmith had informed me that she doesn't "teach," but I didn't believe her. She does ask questions, lots of them, and she seems to know what a child is feeling before he or she gives any obvious external signals.

10:05—Bundled in a red coat with a black hat/scarf wound around her head, she arrives at a playground to supervise recess for the kindergarten through sixth grade children from the five classrooms at her end of the hall. Repeatedly she tries to steer the children away from the magnetic attraction of a huge mud puddle. "Boys, you may not tackle, it's too dangerous," she informs a group of soccer-playing boys and girls. She first asks a reckless child to sit near her and later if he thinks he can control himself. "I think so," he says, watching the ballplayers from a distance. Now children are pretending to fish in the mud puddle with strings tied to sticks.

10:30—Rosy-cheeked boys and girls filter back into the room, and esconced in the rocking chair, Mrs. Goldsmith doles out graham crackers to reaching hands. "Put your stick away, Sara. Sara, try to find a safe place for your stick," and the girl slides it into the chairless leg hole of her teacher's unused desk.

"I'd like to read the stories you write this afternoon. Todd, I'd like to read yours," she says to a boy who looks like he's still thinking of soccer. During recess she told me again that the work patterns the children had gotten into before Halloween had gone completely awry and no one had been accomplishing much. "We're going into our third group now." A boy brings a paper to the rocking chair where she sits quietly. "You've got a good drawing," she tells him. "One of the best things that could happen is that you find a story." Several girls have made a cozy private place behind a screen. She hands paper to a child and asks another if he wants to do dot-to-dot. He agrees and sits down to work with another boy kibitzing his progress.

With Joan's permission, a parade of three children goes to ask the office for pencils but returns empty-handed. "I guess we'll have to make do. We'll have to use our fingernails to write with, I guess," she says while she sharpens pencil stubs.

10:45—"What am I going to do to help you with that writing?" she asks a child next to her on the couch. Several children cluster around and ask her to write out words they want for their stories. She puts her arm around a girl and speaks privately. "Christy really admires you. When you're fooling around you're teaching her things." They talk quietly, then the teacher says, "Let's see your writing," and the girl hands her a paper. "One day in palm tree land," the teacher reads. "That's a good beginning. What happened there?"

Two boys come in more than fifteen minutes late from recess, but all she says is, "Don and Hal, when you get your coats off I need to see you." A girl asks why and her teacher explains how late they are. Several children loll on the carpet. "Let's see what you're reading," she asks one and he holds up his book. "That's pretty hard," she observes noncommittally, perhaps giving him permission to try something else, perhaps praising him for taking on the challenge. He agrees and keeps on reading. The teacher glances at the books the others are reading, probably making mental notes. There certainly are no reading textbooks or reading groups in this classroom.

10:50—Comfortably settled on the couch, a boy leans against her side and reads aloud. Nearby two other children read selected bits from their books aloud to each other. Finally the tardy boys edge towards her. She takes one look at their angry faces and says, "Don, go back and get your work. Hal, put away that rubber band. Do you have a book? Do you want to go to the library?" He ignores her and she slips the rubber band out of his hand. More children ask for words, then she rummages for something to interest Hal. Eagerly he takes a Clifford the Dog book. Mrs. Goldsmith sinks into the sagging couch again and a stream of children come and go for help or just to chat.

"Luke, it's time to go," she tells the kindergartner. "Naomi, can you take Luke to the bus?" she asks a seven-year-old at loose ends. "Luke, you help Naomi. Tell her where to go."

Helping each other is a subtle, recurring message, and these kids seem to get rare pleasure from the process. From what I have seen today Joan doesn't give responsibility only to those she knows will carry through; responsibility is for all of her young students. Now I can see some of the advantages of having kindergarten through third grade children in a single class. Although I understand how older students can help both younger children and their peers, I had thought the mixture of young ones might be chaotic. Instead it's like having a family of extra helpers. Joan told me she'd wanted fourth graders, too, but it hadn't worked out this year.

She asks the boys late from recess if they've gotten their crackers, gives them some, and then joins a group standing around a girl in tears. "Megan, they didn't know they were your pencils when you left them around," she explains gently. She leads the crying child to the couch and explains to the curious onlookers, "She brought some pencils to school and people didn't know they were hers." Children come and go. "Pet, what's up?" she asks one. "You're having a real hard time settling today."

My sense of time still is doing strange things, but I'm better at guessing how much has passed. Maybe it's because Joan slowed down and settled in one spot. I suspect she's responding to the childrens' level of involvement. When they're constructively busy, she lets them come to her. There's a lot of nonverbal communication here.

11:05—She stands up and explains that she has to check on the two sixth grade visitor-helpers who seem only to be eating their lunches. She tells them they are supposed to be helping, not eating, so perhaps they should go back to their room. Next the teacher helps the still angry playground latecomers reenact what happened outside and tell each other directly what they're feeling. "Did you want to play with it all by yourself?" she asks one. They still look sullen, and she tells them that she wishes they would declare peace.

Sara whirls past and Mrs. Bradley asks if she can see her writing, but when the girl returns the playground conference is still underway. Sara hangs dangerously far upside down over the back of the couch until the teacher steadies her waving legs. "Hal, we've got five minutes to lunch. I want to hear the flute."

11:15—"We'll sing while she's getting her flute." Mrs. Goldsmith plays the piano from a watchful, half-standing position, and some children sing, "A doe is a deer, a female deer . . . ," The flute picks up the melody and the children gather. For a moment the angry boys put their arms on each other's shoulders. On request, the musicians play the University of Michigan Fight Song and the children sing lustily. "Now it's time for lunch," the teacher says, and the children leave in unorganized groups.

11:20—Mrs. Goldsmith chats with the parent volunteer about her daughter, then walks down the corridor to the teachers' kitchen and lounge where adults have collected around the microwave to heat their lunches. Spying the music teacher, she asks if he could let her know what he's working on so she can teach it in her class, too. Mrs. Goldsmith's student teacher sits next to her and they talk about the playground problem and the limited but real power of busy work to calm "hyped-up kids."

I notice that many of the teachers are talking about children, learning, and school activities; others are using the mimeograph machine for afternoon "busy work." There's much less gossip and idle chit-chat than the norm in other teachers' rooms I've been in during the last thirty-plus years.

12:00—Back in her room, four hours after arriving at school, Mrs. Goldsmith reorganizes crayons, blocks, and papers while the children return. She asks the older kids to go to their next group and tells the seven, newly arrived afternoon kindergartners to go to the rug. She talks with them, then leaves the student teacher to read aloud to the young ones. A few older children also stand close and listen.

She moves around the room observing what's happening. "Now you're back to being the working girl of the world," she says to a girl who proudly displays a paper. "What are you doing next?"

12:08—Still floating from child to child, she disappears into an open-doored supply closet and returns with a hardcover blank book she gives Karen. Together they talk about what the child wants to have in her book and the girl decides she's most interested in animals. Another girl has festooned herself with strips of orange tape and others are complaining that she's hogging it all. The teacher asks her to put it away and finally resorts to slipping the roll of tape out of the child's hand.

One of her students waves a toy gun around the room. "Sean, put it back in the other room," she says, "I don't like guns." He turns and disappears.

"No, I'm not mad at you," she reassures a child who is late from lunch, "but I might get scared that something happened to you." She tries to talk with another boy, but soon asks, "Do you want us to leave you alone?" He nods in agreement, and she and her current retinue of four children move away.

Is this how children learn how to learn? Today I can't see any particular subject matter content a given group of children is expected to master. Joan seems to value their involvement in activities they enjoy: writing, reading, asking questions, and even what some might call "play." Most of the activities I see are open-ended.

Mrs. Goldsmith sits next to the girl with the special blank book, and a group gathers around the table to look, ask for words, help, etc.; a kindergartner stands in the back and waves his hand in the air for attention. He trails along as she informs the private bevy of girls that they don't look as if they're working. Finally he asks his question and she gives him a paper. Sara and another girl get permission to work under her desk. "Don't leave a mess under there," she warns.

12:25—She hangs up fallen coats and tells a child who wants a pencil that there must be a pencil-eating monster loose in the room. "David, let's work on your journal," she says forcefully, but the boy slips away.

She puts her arm around Don who's sitting on the couch in deep gloom, and an excited boy rushes up waving a paper. "Mrs. Goldsmith, I did it! I did it!" She congratulates the first grader for solving such complicated "borrowing" problems, then asks him to get more math people together and explain what he's done.

He spies me first, however, throws his arm across my shoulder, and shows me what he's done. I'm truly surprised. To start with, today I had seen no signs of "math" work other than blocks, some games, and a few worksheets. Also, this boy, who made up and solved his own problems, had seemed to me a run-of-the-mill wiggler with no particular powers of concentration. Such are the shortcomings of casual observation.

12:35—Mrs. Goldsmith suggests to the girls under her desk across the room that they don't need that space if they're just playing a game, then she rescues a kindergarten girl who has managed to trap herself in the room's toilet.

She returns to Karen, surrounded now by three other children who are admiring the drawing and title in her formerly blank book. She asks a bearded man next to the playhouse if she can help him, and a little boy in the other class comes out the playhouse door and says hello to his dad. Several older boys noisily shuffle and deal cards. When their teacher leans against the playhouse nearby, the boys lower their sound level but keep the cards moving.

The teacher hands another blank, hardcover book to a girl who has been watching Karen longingly, and the two sit at the table together. Two kindergartners tell her they want to write, too. They have never written before, but they are ready to write now, this minute, they insist. She helps them get paper, hands them pencil stubs, and they sit down at the table.

(Wow! That's a motivational scene a teacher can only prepare for, not predict and certainly not mandate. I wonder what will happen next. Will they actually write something today? Does it make any difference now they say they're ready? Tune in next week, next month...next year?)

12:50—The teacher circles the room once again, straightening this and that as she goes. Three or four children bang on different parts of the piano keyboard and ignore her requests for less noise. Finally she closes the piano lid. "Walter, what are you going to do?" she asks and he picks up a book. "Jack, will you help your sister?" Reluntantly he moves off, "Anna, what about your writing?" and the girl runs off to fetch her paper. While she's gone, the teacher sits down with the cardplayers and onlookers.

1:00—Okay, put away the cards," she says. Several boys say something in return. "Let me be the teacher," she answers, half jokingly, "let me be the teacher."

"Time for music everybody," and the entire class, escorted by their teacher and student teacher, marches off to the music room.

1:05—The two teachers return to their room where they talk about Don and Hal's fight. They wonder how they are going to get clean-up completed and worry about Hal who hasn't been able to settle down. After school he goes to day care where he consistently gets into trouble. They decide that he needs to do something positive each day right before he leaves.

(I wonder what happens in these music classes run by music teachers and the art classes run by art teachers. Joan and her colleagues have said they get tired of interruptions, but, on the other hand they both relish having pieces of time to themselves during the school day and value the work done by the special teachers who have chosen to work in this school. It's not as if the children don't have daily art and music experiences in Joan's room, but the special teachers have a more directed approach.)

1:35—The children back from music, Mrs. Goldsmith sits in the rocking chair and holds the stories handed her. "Does anyone else have a story to read?" Most of the children listen appreciatively to one another's writing as she reads—sometimes she has to ask the author to translate a word. They all laugh at the funny parts. Two of the cardplayers continue to sort their mixed-up decks, but they come over when the teacher reads a book to everyone.

When the book is finished and the children have discussed what they like about the story, she says, "We feel hopeless about this mess. What kind of clean-up do you want today?" Hands shoot up and voices suggest color, alphabetical and other methods before there's some consensus on music. The teacher starts playing a boogie, then switches to the Fight Song. Whenever the pace slows, she changes tune or tempo and the activity increases. Up to two-thirds of the children are picking up, sweeping, and straightening. The piles of cards are tidier and more organized by the minute. "If you're done with clean-up, come back to the rug," she says over her music. A few children sing the many verses of a song that includes the refrain, "No one's perfect and no one ever will be." Although more join in, she looks at the cardpeople and says pointedly, "We really need the second and third graders to sing." The song done, she hands out crackers to those who want them, although one child refuses saying that she doesn't deserve one because she didn't do clean-up. "You don't have to clean up to get a cracker," she's told.

(I'm amazed at this display of the power of music. Joan tells me later that she started out to be a music therapist but found her way into a classroom instead. She also says that a teacher doesn't have to be a musician, that the same effects can be achieved with rhythmic chords or drum beats. I guess it's most important to be tuned into the kids.)

2:05—With teacher help and reminders, the children struggle into coats and backpacks. They will leave for their buses directly from this second scheduled recess. Mrs. Goldsmith has to rescue a few more girls from the toilet. A stuck zipper finally gives to teacher fingers. Don comes back asking for reassurance.

2:20—A parent asks for reprints of articles about education, and while the teacher digs through her files another parent comes in to tell her that the family will be moving. They talk about the boy's glasses which he refuses to wear; both think his eyes may have changed. "He has such a good attitude about himself," Mrs. Goldsmith says. "He's getting to be very outgoing."

"I'm glad you think so," the mother says. Don has to be encouraged to leave for day care.

2:30—Sara is back looking for her lost jacket which the student teacher helps her find in the school lost and found as usual. The teacher finds the reprints and promises to talk to a class the parent teaches. Mrs.

Goldsmith says she regularly sends home reprints about child development and education. Alicia comes back and asks for several words she takes along when she leaves with her mother.

3:00—Most of the children gone, the student teacher and teacher talk about the day. "Let's relax tomorrow. It's Friday," Joan says. "Did you see how the third graders are into 'Poor Little Me'? What can we do?"

She says that after thirty-seven years in the classroom, she has "an overall picture of where we're going, but each year is different. I remember what the kids are doing, and I keep a notebook with a profile about each kid. I write about their style of reading and writing and the ways they learn. With this I can have extensive plans when I have to have a substitute. You really have to trust that the kids are moving in the right direction. The teachers in schools in which the principal has no trust start treating their kids the same way they're treated.

"I'm not behaving typically today," she repeats. "Usually I can stay in one place. The kindergartners can tap me on the shoulder when they need help. When you start with them in kindergarten and stay with them for two or three years, even longer, that's my payoff as a teacher."

I ask her if she has a separate plan each day for each child. How does she know what to do from minute to minute? "In a way. They're all in here," she says and taps her head. "But when it comes to details, things change. For example, I'd promised myself I'd save those empty books for children who knew exactly what they wanted to put in them, but look what happened today. I think about all of them in the middle of the night." I try to imagine twenty-six small children running around her brain. Her student teacher wonders if they're thinking about the same children in the same small wakeful hours of the morning.

4:00—"Today I've got a parent conference at 4:30," she explains on the way to the office. "This isn't a typical day."

My head is spinning as I leave, but Joan gets materials together for her conference and looks almost as fresh as the morning.

Chapter 3

A History and Open Education

Everyone knows about education. Everyone knows about teaching and learning. We were sent to school to learn from specially trained teachers just as we send our children to school to be educated. The child's job is to learn that which is taught.

To complete high school, most American youth spend the equivalent of six full time, nonstop, consecutive years in schools between the first and twelfth grade. (Because their Japanese counterparts are required to spend sixty more days in school each year, by graduation they have been in classrooms for eight nonstop years.)

Just what is being taught and what is being learned in these years of education? Why? For what purpose? Are children empty containers awaiting the knowledge their teachers impart? Is the traditional concept of the "school as a filling station" (Deal and Nolan 1978) accurate and inevitable? In its purest expression, traditional educational authorities see their task as filling their charges with "bodies of information, rules, and values of the past" (Deal and Nolan 1978, 9). Is traditional schooling necessary to produce an educated adult?

Schools are a relatively modern invention. Not too long ago children learned chiefly by watching and imitating their elders. Even today children teach each other skills and attitudes, sometimes with an effectiveness adults decry.

As a democratic nation, we recognize the need to educate all citizens. Because of our nation's size and the diversity of our peoples, each community retains considerable control over its children's educational experiences. Ideally, responsive schools could be designed to meet ever-changing human and societal needs, but usually our schools simply mirror the past instead of keeping up with the dazzling pace of change. We are more comfortable with familiar ideas and cherish our old institutions, however imperfectly they fulfill their promises. Many feel that today's schools should resemble yesterday's, even though today's children will live most of their lives in tomorrow's twenty-first century.

In all social institutions the opinions and attitudes of the traditional majority take precedent over those of the minorities, yet the mix of American education is richly varied. We have a history of experimenting with educational methodologies, of looking for the better mousetrap, for more efficient techniques to transmit skills.

Some educators see children not as empty vessels, but as ceaselessly active, seeking organisms. They know the daydreaming, dawdling child is learning just as the diligent, work-producing child is learning. These teachers and parents realize they are aware of only a fraction of that which a child is learning at any given moment. They value the whole child, the whole living organism, each child's emotions, social relationships, physical characteristics, aesthetic sensibilities, and seeking minds. Some of these individuals—John Dewey, Marietta Johnson, Caroline Pratt, and A.S. Neill, for example—have created nontraditional schools to fit learning experiences to their perceptions of children.

Many of the schools founded in the tumultuous Vietnam epoch faded as fast as they emerged, providing a foundation for later rumors proclaiming their total demise. An open education advocate recently wrote their obituary when he said, "In 1976 open education had met what seems to be the ultimate destiny of all radical education reforms: it simply disappeared" (Henley 1987).

Contrary to popular opinion, however, alternative, free, open education remains alive and well. In 1980 an estimated three million Americans were involved in some kind of public alternative education (Raywid 1983). In a few short years the listings tripled in the directory of the mostly private school membership National Coalition of Alternative Community Schools. (The term "free school," once identified more with political ideology than educational philosophy, is seldom used today.)

The schools described in this book are places for learning in which freedom is valued. The education they work to encourage incorporates the following features of alternative schools, free schools, open education and informal classrooms:

1. The students are active participants in decision making.
2. Their parents are expected to be active partners in education.
3. Teachers and students trust and respect one another.
4. Creativity and curiosity are valued and encouraged.
5. Learning how to learn is more important than specific content.
6. Educational goals include self-responsibility and independent learning.
7. Students and/or their parents choose to attend the schools.

This book is about real schools and real people, their successes and problems, their dreams and realities. We will focus on seven schools, three private and four public, which span preschool through high school. All but one are in full operation today in southeast Michigan. Each differs from others in its community. Chart 1 summarizes a few facts about them.

The ideological premises of schools are shaped from a raw mixture of theoretical ideals, the personalities of those involved, and the problems they struggle to address. The structure of each school, the shape of days, is built on a many-faceted foundation.

The schools we shall meet grew out of dissatisfaction with traditional approaches but rest upon different philosophical foundations. Even more varied are the ways in which they came into being.

Two issues will be discussed in detail in the next two chapters. One is philosophical and deals with the goals and purposes of the schools we shall visit. The other is practical and concerns the processes and actions through which the schools came into existence. The two questions are, Why? and How?

The failures of many experimental schools may stem directly from the manner in which they answered the Why? question. Like-minded parents got together and declared, "We don't want our children to suffer from education as we did." With firm conceptions of what they did not want, but with few positive goals or realistic notions of what would take place from day to day, they started schools.

Successful alternative schools are grounded on well-defined philosophies and clear goals (Case 1981). When an institution is wracked by internal dissension, a happening as inevitable as death and taxes when students, parents, and teachers share authority, the antagonists must revisit their goals and purposes. Successful schools implement their

CHART 1
Description of Schools in 1984

School	Status	Ages or Grades of Students	Enrollment Spring 1983	Multi-Age Grouping	Separate Buildings	Own Administrator	Year Started
Clonlara	Private	Ages 2 1/2 to 16	55	Yes	Yes	Yes	1967
Open Classroom Program	Public	Grades 1 to 6	256	Yes	No	No	1982*
Middle Years Alternative	Public	Grades 7 and 8	94	No	No	No	1976
Natural Bridge	Private	Ages 10 to 15	28**	Yes	Yes	Yes	1974
Region Four Open School	Public	Grades K to 8	415	Yes	No***	Yes	1972
Upland Hills Farm School	Private	Ages 5 to 14	52	Yes	Yes	Yes	1971
Community High School	Public	Grades 9 to 12	293	Yes	Yes	Yes	1972

*Since 1971 open or informal classrooms have been available in some neighborhood schools.
**Closed 1980.
***Building shared with traditional program, but areas are separate.

philosophies daily, even if they may not live up to their ideals each minute of the day.

Open Classroom Program, Ann Arbor, Michigan, 1984

A single-story, typical 1950s construction, public elementary school surrounded by comfortable single-family homes hugs large, grassy playing fields. With nineteen classrooms and a capacity of 400 students, the school looks very quiet, its eleven acres of playgrounds deserted. By parent demand, five of the classrooms have been designated open, as have five more in a similar building on the other side of town. Under pressure, supposedly as an experiment, the Ann Arbor School Board has allowed 260 willing children enrolled by lottery to experience this strange, "permissive" environment where most textbooks are seen as stultifying, where children are valued for themselves, not their production.

Doris Sperling jumps up to meet her twenty-eight third, fourth, and fifth graders as they return from their hour with the art teacher. A father who is a regular parent volunteer watches amid the cages of snakes, mice, rats, and guinea pigs, the shelves of books grouped by subject matter, and the tangle of student work stations. Outside the classroom the children must follow the traditional school rules, but inside they make their own traditions. Talking quietly, the boys and girls settle on cushions, chairs, and carpet for their morning meeting. On the agenda is a complaint from the building principal that Open Classroom students have been roaming the halls during lunch period without proper hall passes. The problem is forgotten, however, in the torrent of student questions about why Japanese educators and parents are interested in them and their classroom.

At 11 A.M. a new student teacher wants the children to work on a ditto sheet she has made up. For the student teacher's edification—learning by experience being not only for children—Mrs. Sperling has told her to go ahead. "Listen while I read the directions," the young woman says, then changes her mind and distributes the papers without further directions. Four boys and a girl carry their papers to the cages where they try to tempt a garter snake with a juicy earthworm. Two girls let handfuls of baby white mice run around their arms and over their laps. One boy complains that it's too noisy and asks to work at a desk in the hall. Several children go to their work stations, start to write, and ask for help when they need it. The noise level increases, but only a few children quiet when Mrs. Sperling asks them to be considerate of others. Suddenly the teacher turns off the overhead light and everyone freezes in silence, almost as if they are playing "Statues." It's time for lunch. After the children leave, the student teacher says she won't try giving everyone the same assignment again.

By school board directive, across town the Open Classroom students are being subjected to an extra encounter with the California Achievement Tests. When Rick Hall's twenty-six fifth and sixth graders finish a section, they run outside into the cold spring sunshine. Mr. Hall helps a boy put three young goslings in their swimming pond, the classroom's stainless steel sink. Between tests Lovey Bradley's twenty-nine third and fourth graders celebrate a birthday. Each child ices and decorates their own cupcake, but three boys forget about cake in the excitement of sharing the comic books they are making. Another boy studies a math textbook but everyone sings the Happy Birthday song.

Middle Years Alternative, Ann Arbor, Michigan 1984

Baseball fields, a football field, and three tennis courts reach far into the distance from a multi-windowed concrete block building where ninety-four of the 620 public intermediate school students have chosen to attend this program within a school. The seventh and eighth grade Middle Years Alternative (MYA) has a battered philosophy and four teachers, one each in English, Social Studies, Math, and Science. The remainder of school courses are taught by traditional teachers.

The school bell rings and the hallways fill with a sea of swarming, touching, talking students. Archie and Josh scurry to English with their fellow MYA eighth graders. In Liz Henry-Veeneman's class they talk between mini-episodes of writing. Archie says he's writing a science fiction novel, at least two hundred fifty pages, but Josh points out he's finished only a page and a half so far. Josh is looking at a mimeographed sheet in search of an idea for a project analyzing the communications in advertising. Each of the twenty students has a different activity; most are talking.

Two halls away, Dan Miextyn's eighth grade MYA Social Studies students have asked for a group discussion instead of their customary individual work. Today they are supposed to decide from eyewitness accounts, newspaper stories and other timely records, who fired the first shot of the American Revolution. The teacher takes a vote to determine if the majority wants a discussion, then sits on an empty student desk and organizes a class activity he didn't know would take place.

Books are better than cake in Ann Arbor's Open Classroom Program. Photograph by Alex Korn.

Ann Arbor's Open Classroom Program (now the Bach Open School) and Middle Years Alternative are the results of many years of persistent parental pressure. In the late 1960s parents and teachers independently were excited by reports of the "new" education, including Joseph Featherstone's 1967 description of British informal education in *The New Republic*. In Ann Arbor's intellectual climate, Parents for Alternative Learning Situations (PALS) met regularly to discuss innovations in education and create plans of action. Teachers joined them and began to experiment in their own classrooms.

From 1971 to 1975 the number of designated informal classrooms multiplied from six to thirty-six and were attended by almost nine hundred children. Ninety-five percent of parental requests for placement of their children in such classrooms in their neighborhood schools were being honored when the school board hired its third school superintendent in five and a half years and charged him with bringing order to the town's educational chaos. The number of elementary age students was declining, and when requests for informal classroom placements were at an all-time high, a hostile school board enacted a policy declaring single-graded classrooms the preferred and best forum for instruction. The argument was that students from the multi-age informal classrooms were required to prevent students in two different grades from sharing traditional classrooms. Immediately fewer than half the requests for this program of choice were honored. Then a highly structured reading management system was mandated for all elementary classrooms, and by 1981 only the shadowy fragments of five identified informal classrooms remained—ironically allowing the traditional students and teachers in three schools the "luxury" of single-graded rooms.

Battered but not defeated, parents and teachers continued a more sophisticated fight, first for a school board policy statement declaring that educational alternatives had a right to exist, then for an elementary program. Thousands of people hours were spent in meetings with like-minded teachers and parents and usually opposed school officials and school board members. Because members of PALS were tagged as quintessential troublemakers, a nameless group fought with words, copy machines and telephones. Conforming to the guidelines of the school board's own Policy on Alternative Education, the Open Classroom Program got reluctant approval in 1982. To make sure the upstart educational reformers could not outnumber the traditional majority within a school, the program was split between the two schools you have seen as a two year experiment. There was no kindergarten but students from the entire city could make application and be provided transportation to one of the two sites.

By the second year only a third of the students vying for the 260 allotted places were admitted in the spring lottery. This "lottery for children's lives," as some parents called it, exemplified their image of heartless school administrators. Finally, after the adamantly opposed superintendent resigned, the program was recognized as a full-fledged alternative by a more tolerant school board for whom the open education advocates had waged a vigorous campaign.

The beleaguered open classroom teachers had been working for years without significant administrative support; often they were in subdued conflict with their building principals. Beholden to idealistic and energetic parents, they struggled to maintain their own classrooms, and an interactive, integrated program remained only a dream. The children of parents who had fought longest and hardest did what all children do; they grew up, ironically most without benefit of the educational program their parents fought for.

With a new superintendent came new possibilities. In 1986 major efforts to racially balance elementary school populations resulted in children being moved and buildings closed. An eccentric building with gargoyles on the ramparts and a chaotic layout became the new Open School, complete with its own principal. Typically there was controversy about the school building and the principal, but more of this turnabout tale will be found in the final chapter.

The Middle Years Alternative program was a logical outgrowth of the informal classrooms. Some parents wanted their children to continue with compatible intermediate or middle school education, while others whose neighborhood schools lacked informal classrooms wanted an open enrollment, district-wide intermediate program. MYA was approved by the school board in 1976 after three years of embattled meetings. With students enrolled and teachers selected by parents and students, MYA began as a four classroom experimental pilot program.

In its early days MYA had the multi-age classrooms, integrated subject matter, and student and parent participation in curricular decisions which characterized the informal classrooms. Then the staff changed. Ann Arbor's standards for academic specialization and the demands of a new (and relatively short-lived) intermediate school curriculum worked against generalized education. Soon the MYA teachers retreated to single-grade, basic subject classrooms in which students were allowed to select activities from a teacher-determined menu.

School administrators have said the program was hastily conceived and poorly considered, but in its second planning year the originating PALS committee had been assigned representatives from central administration, teachers and principals, and together they spent the next year appearing before assorted public school committees. The program's ultimate weakness lay not in the planning, but the implementation.

Sympathetic and philosophically knowledgeable teachers for students this age were (and are) surprisingly hard to find. One excellent high school teacher became an unhappy intermediate school teacher in the position which she had requested. Most teachers seem to prefer working with pliable younger students or more "intellectually stimulating" older ones, not the hormonally unstable ones in the middle.

Started as an experiment, the MYA program was slated for termination as soon as enrollment dropped below a given number on either of two dates a year. It is hard enough for students to leave their friends and home schools, but to take that risk along with the risk that the program would be cancelled in midterm was excessive. Enrollment did not grow and stabilize until assurances were given that the program would last through the year, regardless of interim attendance.

Open or Informal Education

This battle for an educational ideology is remarkable even in Ann Arbor, a university community well-acquainted with militant idealism. What were they fighting for? Cynical administrators have been heard to say that these parents were only elitists in militant's clothing, that all they wanted were the "best" teachers for their children. It would have been far simpler, however, for these parents to start their own private school and hire their own teachers than to struggle against odds to change the public system. What they wanted was public education based on the model of British informal education.

A primary goal of open education is that children be respected as whole, indivisible humans, as people who develop and learn in interaction with their total environment, from classroom to community. The resulting learning environment is light years away from the traditional educational "filling station." Teachers are helpers and guides instead of authorities. Because learning is continuous, parents have significant roles to play. Multi-age classrooms expand the learning opportunities.

Learning is experiential and integrated, the pace and pattern determined by students in cooperation with their teachers. Time and space are open. Individuals are their own competition and are not compared by letter grade or test score with others.

"Important goals of the Open School," the Detroit Open School brochure states, "are the growth of independent thinking and development of a positive self-concept. A positive self-concept will help an individual 'make it' whatever should happen. Those who become independent thinkers will continue to learn in any future situation."

Critics claim that the goals of traditional and open education are the same and that the mollycoddling practices of open education should not be tolerated. Yet the practices, the shared decision making, the mutual trust and respect, the multiple resources, are a tangible expression of the goals.

A student teacher experienced in the ways of traditional education found herself placed in a combined first and second grade open classroom and jotted down the differences she saw between the different forms of education.

- The pace is quicker—there are lots of mini-lessons and mini-units.
- Learning is spontaneous—different people bring different experiences to the group and can provide a new perspective.
- Children can further personal interests in an independent manner.
- It is more of a class-free environment—students are less concerned with levels.
- So many things are going on at once in the classroom that learning can be switched from one subject to another in a shorter period of time.
- It is flexible. If the students have a better idea than the one the teacher has offered, they are encouraged to express it.
- More geared toward everyone being a student and teacher at some point.
- Children set personal goals and try to compete with themselves instead of one another.

This student teacher was not in Joan Goldsmith's classroom, but another in Ann Arbor. The similarities are remarkable, but open education is attractive to a wider range of the population than those drawn to an intellectually idealistic university town.

Five years after riots had decimated much of downtown Detroit, open education came to this gritty, determined industrial city.

Region Four Open School, Detroit, Michigan, 1983

A towering yellow-brown brick chimney rises factory-like above the ugly building squatting behind a wire fence on blacktop and bare mud.

Region Four Open School, a faded, crayoned sign reads above the wire covered glass doors. Inside 275 elementary and 140 middle Open School students share the building with 140 traditional Burgess School students, each in their own territory. The exposed pipes, ancient metal lockers and concrete block walls in the Open School wings are painted rainbow colors, and children's art and children are everywhere.

In its ten years the program has moved six times to different buildings, but so many parents want their children to attend that they wait in line, day and night, up to twelve full days to gain admission. The parents, students, and teachers come in all colors; the majority are black.

The thirty-two third and fourth grade students inside Diana Kennedy's open classroom door are busy. Five girls are counting money for next year's field trips, money raised by the children for their own public school activities. On a table underneath a mounted science project titled, "Energy from Lunch," three boys are helping each other write. "I want to learn how to draw," writes Rodrigues. "My grandmother could teach me."

"Before the end of the school year," Kwami writes, "I need to work on multiplication." Earlier in the day the children brainstormed ideas about what they want to accomplish in the six weeks remaining before the long summer vacation.

A mother with a cast on her broken foot and a toddler in tow breathlessly pops into Laurajean Milligan's crowded multi-purpose office. She says she's really upset. After she had gotten up her nerve and volunteered to be in the performance for the school's ten year anniversary party, no one had called her. The school director apologizes for the oversight and assures her that she's welcome. "We need everyone! Thanks for stopping and letting us know."

The Region Four Open School (today the Detroit Open School with a building to itself) has been a success in all its forms since its 1972 beginnings. The reason for its success may be the good fortune by which a former kindergarten teacher with direct experience in British informal education became its first and, to date, only director.

In the upheavals surrounding the beginnings of these schools, Detroit decentralized its school management. A Region Four School

Board member somehow heard of something called open education and, although he wasn't sure what it would look like, decided he wanted a school like that in his district. The board member used his personal power to politic at the money-controlling city level, and in time the school was ordered into existence. Almost by chance, an elementary school principal heard about the directive and remembered one of his kindergarten teachers who had actually taught in British informal classrooms.

Laurajean Milligan says that except for her trips to England she had been teaching kindergarten "almost forever. For some reason I'd gotten a reputation among parents for being a good teacher." Her principal asked her to start a kindergarten through third grade program just for his school, with teachers willing to try something new. The program attracted a large following from the first. The Region Four Board saw the success and next year wanted the program available to all children. Amidst anguish from those left behind, Laurajean and her staff moved to another building, but demand continued to exceed the capacity of staff and building.

The summer before the regionwide school opened, Laurajean Milligan and one of her staff traveled at their own expense to England. Because English school calendars are not based on our agrarian schedule, they were able to visit fifteen different schools in operation. "Fourteen were terrific and one was lousy," Laurajean says. "We learned from all of them." The significance of their curiosity and travels cannot be underestimated. While the teachers at our other schools had to struggle to turn written words into action, not one, but two of the Region Four Open School staff had experienced the successes and failures of open education. Their leadership and vision have built a school with a unified purpose, with teachers who relate as colleagues to create an integrated educational environment.

This school has survived twenty-nine burglaries, but others in Detroit have had worse. It has moved six times, usually for purposes more political than educational. When one building caught on fire, the parents who heard the late night news turned out in wintery cold to rescue the books and equipment from their school. Although the Open School has nominal administrative support, or at least not active hostility, it suffers from benign neglect. The system is not geared to providing many copies of different story books instead of sets of textbooks with matching workbooks. Overstuffed cushions and two-story lofts are not on traditional requisition inventories. A school which doesn't hand out report cards with grades is an anomaly in this system.

Parents have learned to exercise sophisticated and united political pressure to maintain the flexibility and support required for a successful program. They insisted that higher grades be added as the children got older. At first the grade six through eight middle school was kept separate, but eventually it came under the same roof as the elementary school. Student turnover is close to zero. Although demand is so great that any number of buildings could be filled with open education, enrollment has been limited by the Detroit School Administration. For mysterious reasons, it took eleven years for Laurajean Milligan to be recognized and paid as the veteran administrator she is.

At the well-attended tenth year reunion, parents and teachers vented their frustration in a song to the tune of "Second Hand Rose."

> We are in a school, strictly second hand
> Everything from toothpicks to a baby grand.
> Stuff in all our classrooms has been used before.
> Even things we're reading
> Someone read before.
> It's no wonder that we feel abused
> We never had a thing that ain't been used.
> We're using second hand books, tables and chairs,
> If they don't want it
> They send us theirs.
> Even our piano in the common room
> Was sent by mistake . . .

These are sentiments echoed in all our schools where teachers are imaginative packrats who collect "stuff" for their students wherever they go.

We now meet four more schools founded with different philosophical emphases.

Chapter 4

CHILD-DIRECTED AND COMMUNITY-ORIENTED SCHOOLS

Open classroom teacher Joan Goldsmith said her real payoff came when she could start with fresh kindergartners free of preconceptions about the nature of school learning and keep them in her class for several years. These children would be able to grow and pick up skills in their own time as they learned both from other children and from a teacher sensitive to their developmental needs. Although the open school teacher's role is subtle and low keyed, he or she ultimately assumes the responsibility for each child's broad-based education. The teacher must both trust the child and provide an environment which stimulates the child. It is a difficult balancing act.

While overlapping the philosophical premises of open education, two of our schools may go further than the open schools in giving responsibility to their young students.

CHILD-DIRECTED

The private Clonlara and Upland Hills Farm Schools most closely exemplify a philosophy of education described as "the school as a garden" (Deal and Nolan, 1978). If only children can be allowed to grow naturally, its advocates believe, they will develop and build upon their innate goodness. A. S. Neill proposed that children were filled not with original sin, but with "original joy."

In its purest form,this type of school provides an atmosphere in which students are completely free to choose their own activities, to schedule their own time, and to create their own environments with an absolute minimum of adult interference.

Clonlara, Ann Arbor, Michigan, 1983

Two old wood frame houses, blue and green, and two ancient trailer type portable classrooms take little space on this two-and-a-half acre wooded lot.

In 1967 ex-nun Pat Montgomery opened an eight-child private preschool which has expanded to include fifty-five students from two-and-a-half to sixteen years old.

This April morning is the first day for a new student. Twelve-year-old Taka Yamamoto's head must be spinning, for only thirty-six hours ago he had been in his hometown of Nara City, Japan. Now he's in a portable classroom surrounded by a handful of Clonlara students. "Mouth." says blonde Jason pointing at his own ever talking lips. Taka smiles and nods.

"Aha," says John, picking up a carved wooden dragon. "He'll know what this is." It's like an English language treasure hunt. On his first day of American school, Taka speaks almost no English and no staff member or student speaks Japanese.

Ignoring the chatter, a tall boy has folded himself up by a computer as he attempts to land his computer plane safely. The computer and its television screen are hung with signs admonishing prospective users to take lessons from Jon before placing a finger to key. The eleven-year-old son of the parent who donated the computer has more expertise than anyone else in the school, including teachers, and so has become an instructor.

Crammed bookshelves line two parts of the room. Ramona, thirteen, looks very maternal as she sits on a couch and reads aloud to two girls her age. Pia Emrick, a teacher smaller than many of her students, confers quietly with a mother and daughter. Another girl sits with them, her straying blonde hair hiding her face. With radarlike skill, Pia's brown eyes track the different activities while she concentrates on the conversation.

In the front portable volunteer teacher Julia and a fifteen-year-old

Clonlara student are looking at books with two of the young children. A seven-year-old flies a pretend plane made of two sticks tied together. "Do you want to fly it now?" Kyla asks Carley who has been watching with yearning blue eyes. Three other children are building a city with big wooden blocks. Since the weather is fine, Brian, seven, and several others are inside and out; they climb the jungle gym, swing from the trees, and dart in and out of their classroom to see if they're missing anything.

In the Blue House, the preschoolers eat their early lunch with their teacher, Ken.

Pat Montgomery describes the ideal teacher/child relationship at Clonlara as similar to that between twenty-one-year-old friends. Expressing emotions honestly is of highest value. Students and teachers are equals living together, solving social problems by group process, and, when the time is right, attending or teaching traditional skill and subject matter classes. This is the education "without compulsion" for which the Japanese yearned.

Clonlara is a school started by a single individual, and in Pat Montgomery's thirty-plus years of dispensing education her philosophy has changed profoundly. At eighteen she was a teaching nun in a Catholic school. She left the convent in her midtwenties but continued teaching in public schools. After marriage and two children, she and her husband were faced with the revelation that their daughter and son would have to go to school and that they did not want them to attend any school vaguely resembling those in which Pat had taught. It was this very personal problem that led her to A.S. Neill's book, *Summerhill* (1960), and then to Leiston, England for a three-week visit to the school deemed outlandish by some and revered by others.

The need behind Clonlara was humane education of her own and all children. The inspiration came from A.S. Neill, an old man who encouraged Pat to start her own school, a charismatic old man who lectured her, "Don't imitate or be a disciple of anyone. There's a school in each of us waiting to start. Let that one begin."

On return, Pat opened a nursery school for eight three- and four-year-olds. The effort was financed entirely with money her husband was able to borrow; Pat was the unpaid teacher.

With the annual addition of the next older age group the nursery school became an elementary school. Gradually parents and salaried staff members began to participate in decision making. This group effort was new to everyone, and Pat remembers it as a time when the blind were leading the blind. Mired in inexperience, everyone struggled and learned painfully. It is in these early days that a school may sink or swim while its participants test their lofty ideals against cold realities.

Clonlara has survived a fire which destroyed one of its two buildings. Its financing remains a tangle of loans and timely miracles. The students have come and gone while Pat Montgomery has stayed, still unpaid, in a changing role. Today a parent/student/staff board (about which more will be said later) makes policy decisions, tries to stimulate fund-raising, and hires and fires staff. Overall the school looks the same, but the nursery school children are gone, their play space filled with file cabinets and desks from which Pat helps parents teach their children at home. Home schooling, the ultimate in individualized instruction, is appealing to many American parents who want to control all aspects of their children's learning environments; even some school phobic Japanese children are being helped by Clonlara's home schooling program. Today the home schooling movement takes all Pat's time and energy, and she has become almost as familiar with judges and courtrooms as classrooms.

The hows of Clonlara's school organization have changed over the years, but the goals have remained intact. Learning to live with other people and to take responsibility for one's own actions is much more important than math or reading. The children at Clonlara neither follow adult-made rules nor study only that which adults say they must. The actual style of teaching often is traditional, however, reflecting Neill's comment about Summerhill: "We have no new methods of teaching because we do not consider that teaching itself matters very much" (Deal and Nolan 1978, 32). Each student is valued as a unique individual; the school's goal is that the child grows as a whole person, undivided, much more complex and complete than a head stuffed with learning.

The staff at Upland Hills Farm School also is convinced that all children are geniuses equipped at birth with talents and gifts only waiting to unfold. The educator's task is to draw out each child's natural tendencies. The staff says that the basic skills of self-intelligence and self-knowledge cannot be taught and the educator only can create an environment where it will occur.

Upland Hills Farm School, Oxford, Michigan, 1983

Two windmills, a geodesic dome, and a scattering of other buildings sit among rolling hills on a working farm. The windmills hum steadily in the spring wind while the fifty-two children, aged five to fourteen, sort themselves into five groups for the first meeting of the day.

Since it first opened in 1971, Upland Hills Farm School has become energy self-sufficient. Six-year-old Katie Yamasaki's architect father helped design the plans. Each person, student or teacher, is aware of his or her interrelationship with the environment.

The school's director, Phil Moore, meets in the geodesic dome with the oldest students to discuss the choices each has that day. "Will there be time to study?" Suzy asks. "I need to study." This need is fueled by the fact that the oldest students are subjected to final exams in preparation for the realities of the traditional schools they soon will be attending. No other students at Upland Hills are tested, and four veteran students in the equivalent of the eighth grade will be taking the first formal exams of their school lives. Phil leads the students in a discussion of some of the test subjects; they include Canadian geography, Great Britain, Buckminster Fuller, and Ghandi.

In each group students select their own daily activities from a menu of choices. Today ten students, including five-year-old Marla and twelve-year-old Tom, have decided they want to go to the farm with teacher Ken Webster. The teacher takes photographs of the children with the farm animals, and next week they will meet to write captions for their pictures. Tom and Marla try to gather enough courage to feed a pony while Mark leaps on a sheep's broad, fleecy back. The teacher orders Mark off, right now, no arguments.

Because a play is scheduled for public performance next week, the student actors know they should go to rehearsal, not the farm, but still they are given the choice to make. The day is broken into three periods, each with four possible choices of activity. At the end of the day the students meet again with their group for a period of self-evaluation.

The young people at Upland Hills Farm School move from activity to activity without direction or bells. Perhaps they read time from the sun. They learn from, and their learning is reinforced by, practical, multisensory experiences. At Upland Hills one feels a definite repeating rhythm, almost like the changing of seasons or the movement of the earth.

After a tumultuous beginning, this school's essence, its whys, have been well-defined, but like the others, the daily processes aimed at reaching the goals constantly are reshaped. The school opened in the ground level of a barn; it was the creation of a university professor of education, the farm-owning parents of a five-year-old, and other interested parents. As the first year progressed it was clear that their idealistic visions had not become reality. The planners had little idea of how to replace the repressive educational horrors they abhorred with the energy and creativity they yearned for.

At the end of the first year all the staff but Phil Moore quit, and the school started anew. Phil collected a staff bonded by friendship, if not by training in education. The friends took on the uneasy task of creating a stable educational environment in which children already hurt by "education" would regain their courage and strength and those new to schooling would develop freely.

The thinking of Jiddu Krishnamurti and Margaret Mead continues to influence the school's goals and aspirations, and Jean Piaget its practices. Phil's teacher and mentor, the unclassifiable Buckminster Fuller, provided inspiration and practical ideas reinforced by visits to the school. His motto, "Think globally, act locally," underscores Phil's many activities including speaking tours in Europe and South Africa.

Of the private schools, Upland Hills has been most free of the constant, dragging concern about how to meet a payroll and pay for rent and insurance. (The problems of school financing will be addressed in a more leisurely fashion further on.)

The staff first proved they could create a loving learning environment where children would flourish without damage, then realized they wanted more. Secure that the students' emotional and social needs were being met, they set themselves the task of exciting them with learning, of helping them become agents of societal change.

STUDENTS IN THE COMMUNITY

Our last two schools were created specifically for older students and were founded on the premises that young people should be active members of society and that both student learning and society would benefit in the process. Deal and Nolan describe this ideology as the "school as a marketplace." The emphasis is on experience, on students experimenting and solving real problems. In large part this philosophic foundation grows from the progressive movement which flowered in the 1930s. Student transactions in this "negotiation school" may involve social and personal beliefs, values, and information.

Although this kind of education emphasizes direct experience, not the lectures and textbooks with which the traditional teacher fills student heads, John Dewey pointed out that all experiences are not educative. "Experience and education cannot be directly equated with each other," he stated, "for some experiences are miseducative. Any experience is miseducative that has the effect of arresting or distorting the growth of further experience" (Deal and Nolan 1978, 27).

Natural Bridge School, Tallahassee, Florida, 1978

A two-story white frame house on a small city lot is dwarfed by palm trees and a two-century-old live oak tree trailing garlands of Spanish moss.

Long before the arrival of any sleepy-eyed adult, Lynda and Clay unlock the school door with the key on the porch. Black-whiskered T.S. Eliot twines through their legs and meows to be fed. By 8:45, twenty-eight young people, ten to fifteen years of age, and three of their elders have gathered in the former living room for group meeting.

The thirteen-year-old group leader tries to find a resolution to a teacher's complaint that students are late to his classes. "You're late, too, Terry," Jenny points out to her teacher. "You're not being fair."

A boy says Natural Bridge should have a bell like other schools. A girl in bare feet and blue jeans says she could bring a handbell from home but that she'd never ring it.

"Even with a bell, which I don't want, we still have too many things to do," another boy says. "Maybe we could start school earlier or end it later." After thirty minutes of discussion, all but one dissenter vote to extend the school day by fifteen minutes in the afternoon, and group meeting is over.

Three students are dropped off by a parent driver at their volunteer work at a convalescent home. Two others pretend to study Russian, a subject they requested but have mixed feelings about. Three boys ride bikes around the house on a track they built. Alex and Kate find paints and brushes and work on their wall paintings. Others go to classes or sit and talk, usually after grabbing food from their lunchbags.

At Natural Bridge there is little of the calm of Clonlara or Upland Hills. The school tingles with early adolescent energy.

This scene from history describes a school which no longer exists, one which closed its doors only six years after being opened by an individual. Two years after I, its founder, moved a thousand miles north, Natural Bridge collapsed from lack of 1) energy and 2) cash. Schools birthed by a philosophically congenial group have built-in survival power, but those started by an individual are vulnerable to the loss of that person.

Although I founded a school, I'd never had the slightest desire of being a traditional school teacher. After many years as a psychotherapist, researcher, school psychologist, and university teacher, I found myself middle-aged, in a new community, and out of work. After many years of working with children, I was convinced there had to be better ways to provide education. After all, if school environments were truly responsive to the developing needs of the young, psychotherapists might have empty waiting rooms.

I was committed to public education, but the public schools neither wanted to employ me nor put my ideas into practice. And so I planned to build a private school. Once it was a functioning reality I was sure the public system would take it in. Although many public school teachers sent their children to be educated in this private school and more came to observe its antics, Natural Bridge did not become a public institution.

I had seen many of the local public elementary schools and knew that some were blessed with excellent teachers and principals. The middle schools, however, like many of their counterparts in the rest of the nation, could be actively destructive. Students turned against teachers, against learning, and against their peers. So Natural Bridge would be for students in the middle, including my son for a time, for those volatile people balancing between adult and child.

The goals of awakening interests, of keeping student options open, of learning how to learn, of respecting and trusting the entire person, of making a difference, were not original or new. John Dewey's writing had great impact, but ideas which shaped daily school life came from many sources including J. McV. Hunt and Jean Piaget. Learning experiences would be experiential and multi-dimensional, often shaped by the experts the students in the middle admired.

Advertisements drew parents and teachers to free bank meeting rooms to hear about the idea school. After a year of planning discussions, of money grubbing, of finding a building, hiring two certified teachers, and contending with armies of disapproving building inspectors, Natural Bridge opened with twenty students and enough cash to survive one frugal year.

We soon found that outlining beautiful educational goals was simpler than dealing with reality. Usually off-balance, we found ourselves swinging pendulum-like between extreme permissiveness and old authoritarian habits. Students had to learn that they could accept the responsibility that the staff could relinquish. Group meeting was the negotiation point from which most action came. The hows of education, the procedures, constantly were re-created, most effectively with the active participation of the perceptive students. The students always were the center of focus and the balancing pole for the staff. Each new year was easier than the last as we learned together. Closing this school which had changed us all was painful.

Community High School, Ann Arbor, Michigan, 1984

A three-story red brick winged rectangle is centered on a grassy knoll; a gold lettered sign over the double front doors upgrades the battered exterior. Community High School is housed in a sixty-year-old building once closed as unfit for elementary students. Since 1972, space available, any Ann Arbor student in grades nine through twelve has been able to choose to attend Community instead of one of the other two large traditional high schools.

The 293 students won't be found together in the building at any one time, however. Outside the front door a longhaired boy swoops back and forth on a skateboard while two friends examine a parked motorcycle. A girl with pink and blue punk rock hair laughs at a friend adorned with a blacklapelled white tuxedo jacket, faded blue jeans, and a khaki hat.

Inside, ponytailed Jeff sits with his friends on a hallway brick bench and looks stunned when he's asked to describe the typical Community High student. "I guess you could say we're all either male or female," he says with a straight face. "Yeah, that's right," his friends agree. After a pause Jeff adds, "What we probably all have in common is that we came here for more freedom."

Biology teacher Mike Mouradian stands in front of his fifteen students while a girl sits at her teacher's desk. Over the door an image of Albert Einstein irreverently sticks out his tongue. A boy saunters in late and makes a face when he learns that today he'll have to dissect an earthworm. His teacher laughingly assures him that he'll like it.

A yellow shuttle bus pulls up behind the building, more or less on schedule, to transport students to classes at the traditional high schools. Community is too small to offer a full range of courses, so some students elect to take classes at the schools they have chosen not to attend full-time.

The entire community is a classroom for these students who also learn new skills and attitudes and earn credits for graduation by working in a photographer's studio or a gas station or a print shop. The school's community resource catalogue lists almost two hundred ways to earn academic credit outside regular courses, but 60 percent of the community

Typical hall-sitters at Community High School. Photograph by Alex Korn.

resource courses are created by the students themselves. They decide what they want to learn, find their own volunteer teacher, and work out a contract with one of the two teachers in the Community Resource Office.

Julie sits in the hallway wearing an astonishing short white dress covered entirely with long silk fringe and blue sequins which match her tennis shoes and eye shadow. She says that last semester she got an A in a junior level University of Michigan course titled Medieval Sources of Modern Culture, a course she had talked her way into without registering and for which she received high school credit.

A few students from the traditional high schools take advantage of the community resource program.

Here there are many choices, many ways to learn, and no school bells.

"Community High School is a four-year, cross-aged, academic high school which will maximize a student's opportunity to use the community as a source of study," reads the philosophy statement in its 1972 blueprint. "It is designed to offer each student a carefully constructed and monitored program which will capitalize on his interests and address his individual educational needs."

Respect for the whole individual is joined by involvement with the community. Students are seen as problem solvers and philosophers. They enter into negotiations with their teachers and with one another about their learning programs and experiences. Deal and Nolan describe the latter as "tension between what kids want and what they need"; at Natural Bridge we called it "tightrope walking" and it was an exciting business. Community High School was created during the short, colorful tenure of a radical school superintendent charged by the school board to institute change. Bruce McPherson lasted only a year and a half, but the school he opened still survives, recently with increasing demand.

A faculty member from 1972 to 1977 and dean until 1983, Connie Craft answered a newspaper ad offering a job in the highly touted Ann Arbor schools to a person "interested in alternative education," and found that she and 110 others had applied for the last opening on the six person Community High planning team. Asked in an interview how she taught reading, she answered with an honest, "Damned if I know," and got the job. The reforming superintendent brought his own team from Philadelphia, from the same Parkway program the Japanese journalist visited in 1983, from the secondary school without buildings and walls

CHART 2
How They Began

School	Private			Public			
	Clonlara	Natural Bridge	Upland Hills Farm School	Open Classroom	Middle Years Alternative	Community High School	Region Four Open School
Ages of First Students	3 to 4	10 to 15	5 to 15	5 to 12 Grades 1 to 6	12 to 14 Grades 7 and 8	14 to 19 Grades 9 to 12	5 to 9 Grades K to 3
First Enrollment	8	20	45	256*	103	293	415
Age Range	2 1/2 to 16	10 to 15	5 to 14	5 to 12	12 to 14	14 to 19	5 to 14

	A.S. Neil	J. Dewey J. McV. Hunt J. Piaget	Buckminster Fuller, Krishnamurti, Ashley Montague, M. Mead	British Informal Education	British Informal Education	Parkway Program (school without walls)	British Informal Education
Philosophical Sources							
Originator	Single Person	Single Person	Small Group	Teachers and Parents	Parents	School System Committee	School Board Member
Originator's Motivation	Dissatis-faction; Two Small Children	Dissatis-faction	Dissatis-faction	Dissatis-faction; Knowledge of New Ideas	Aging Informal Classroom Students	Student Unrest	Dissatis-faction

*Number Determined by School Board. There are fewer spaces than applications.
**Maximum Enrollment-Cloased 1980.

he and his staff had founded. At Parkway, students learned in the community, and, with modifications, that would be the Ann Arbor plan. Restless and rebellious high school students in Ann Arbor were demanding meaningful learning. They wanted to assume responsibility for themselves and to participate in planning their school.

"We used to get into such arguments," retired teacher Bets Hansen recalls. Ideas for the school were taken to coffees in parents' homes and to all PTO meetings. The committee haunted the traditional high schools and spoke with anyone willing to be seen with them. Representatives of Ann Arbor's power elite were invited to meetings; the Chamber of Commerce was courted.

In May, a conservative school board reluctantly approved the new school, but only if, before the end of the school year, 520 students would commit themselves by enrolling in this idea with neither building nor teaching staff. The superintendent threw a champagne party for the planning committee when the magical number had been reached; then everyone tackled the real problems of opening a school in three short months.

The hardworking students, teachers, and parents were elated at their victory, but the school board members put another twist on it. "We don't want them in our schools. If that's what they want, then we'll pay to get them out," some said. The majority felt they were isolating undesirables in a surplus school building. Students, parents, and the committee all had a voice in staff hiring. The school board provided the promised start-up money—which was enough to pay for required fire escapes but fell short on supplies, bookshelves, paint, and even plaster to patch the holes in the walls. Many years later the school is relatively poorly equipped, a complaint shared by other public alternative programs.

Community High was open to any student who wanted to come. "In the beginning it was bedlam, but exciting bedlam," Bets Hansen remembers. The dissidents and the disillusioned, the bored and the brilliant, the drug using near dropouts, gathered in their school, and, with the staff and parents, set to building bookshelves and plastering and painting the ceilings and walls.

In a reflection of the times, Community has become more conservative, but its reputation has lost none of its color. Outrageous dress and hair styles are the norm, but, terrifying as the school is to outsiders, even a casual visitor is received with warm hospitality; a visit to a traditional high school, where you are surrounded by crowds of oblivious students, is, by contrast, a lesson in invisibility.

The students, parents, and staff are experts at exerting political pressure. They have learned to anticipate and respond effectively to frequent threats. They know the power of jamming school board meetings and speaking up for an educational program they believe in.

Elements of Natural Bridge and Community High are contained in other schools; the difference is in emphasis.

These schools all have visions of their long range goals, but the continuing challenge is inventing the procedures which make them attainable. All the schools continue to experiment as they search for the best methods to meet the needs of their present students. The small private schools have almost unlimited flexibility in creating exciting learning environments but may be handicapped by a lack of resources. Innovative public schools often exhaust their precious energies fighting for existence and are weakened by the compromises necessary for minimal survival.

The early years of a new program or school are bound to be stressful as the students and staff experiment and experience new ways of being. Fortunately young people handily survive such temporary well-intentioned turmoil, possibly better than their elders.

Chapter 5

WHAT AND WHO:
CURRICULUM AND STAFFING

Most of us think of curriculum as an orderly, linear progression of courses or academic tasks separated by subject matter; but in these innovative schools curriculum is a complex process with many interacting dimensions. Their concern with the development of the whole, undivided student means that they emphasize integrated, experiential learning, and place limited value on traditional academic activities.

Their curricula may include multi-dimensional experiences, whetting interests, individual projects, spontaneous happenings, group discussions, travel, and more. Relatively traditional subject matter courses may be open to students of different ages and experience, may be taught by a volunteer or a student, might use textbooks in nontraditional ways, and seldom result in graded outcomes.

Among the characteristics of alternative schools, what Mary Anne Raywid terms "schools of choice," are greater autonomy and freedom from external authorities (Raywid, 1984). Individual teachers such as Joan Goldsmith exert greater control over their educational practices than do their traditional counterparts. Even if some Community High staff members teach relatively traditional courses, the choice is theirs, not a principal's nor a curriculum consultant's. With freedom comes greater responsibility.

In this chapter we will first look at the forces which contribute to the curricula of our innovative schools. The primary emphasis here will be on who determines the curricular activities, although the nearly unlimited range of educational happenings will be glimpsed along the way.

Whatever the nuances of educational philosophy, the teaching staff is responsible for making the individualized and innovative curricula work. We will see the variety of people who bring their skills and energies to these schools and see how teachers are selected.

CURRICULUM: WHO DECIDES?

The first day at Natural Bridge felt like an exhilarating and terrifying free fall into unknown waters. There was no precast curriculum to hand to these young people whose parents had been assured their children would learn. There were no spelling lists graded by difficulty, no reading texts sequentially color coded to multiple choice tests, no sixth, seventh, and eighth grade pass/fail standards.

The students, who came to this school for many different reasons, were to provide the materials for their own curricular foundations. First we had to get acquainted, to learn about one another's interests, needs, feelings, strengths, jokes, and sorrows; then together we shaped our mutual living and learning environment.

A common goal of these innovative schools is the creation of an attractive and comfortable learning environment, or curriculum, if you will, which fits each individual. The staffs realize that no two individuals, even identical twins, process the same experience in exactly the same way.

The curriculum must be flexible and imaginative. It not only must fit a given student at a given time, but also provide the skills and attitudes necessary to meet future individual and societal challenges. Educators actually are fortune tellers who peer eagerly into the crystal ball of the future while engaged in a consuming, demanding present. The curricular boundaries of traditional education are set by past practices, and teachers work to transmit familiar skills and bodies of knowledge to their young charges. They leave the crystal ball problems to designated authorities, but those involved in open, alternative education cannot accept such a passive role. They are excited by the demands and pleasures of curriculum creation.

The curriculum experts in the schools we have seen include the students, the staff, the parents, and in expanding circles, the community and society. Each school achieves its own unique balance between what the students feel they need and the demands of their parents, teachers, and societal forces.

Elementary Years

Clonlara. At Clonlara, the pattern of the days remains recognizable while it continually shifts. The single fixed, immutable star is the group meeting which everyone is required to attend. In these mandatory meetings students and staff talk about everything from their group structure to an individual's problems. While meetings may be scheduled, anyone, at anytime, is entitled to assemble the entire school to help solve a problem.

Each fall at Clonlara, the students and staff spend time getting acquainted; together they explore the possibilities and challenges of a new year. After considering what she or he would like to accomplish and alternative routes to meeting these goals, a student selects a staff member to help outline an individual course of study. This outline then becomes the basis for a parent/student/staff conference from which the plan may emerge intact or greatly altered. In this discussion all participants try to balance curricular concerns.

The State of Michigan provides detailed lists of minimal performance objectives for each grade in every subject matter area from mathematics to art. While these objectives are taken into account in making individual curricular plans at Clonlara, no state official monitors their implementation.

A five-year-old Kyla probably insisted that she wanted to learn how to read. Perhaps she wanted to understand the magic of numbers, too, but she never would have proposed that, "Given sets of one to five small objects as members, will point to the sets that have the same number of objects," as does one Michigan objective. She also would have mentioned that she loved music and wanted to sing and make songs.

At age ten, her curricular goal setting will have become more complicated. She will have been reading for a long time, will still love music and will have found new loves, but the learning goals she will be able to state will be short and discrete. Perhaps she will say, "I want to write a story every week. I will read three books before Thanksgiving and finish the first section of the fifth grade math workbook."

This curricular goal setting process is an absolute mystery to an eleven-year-old newcomer to Clonlara. At first there will be false starts and many changes. Jason might righteously claim, "I'm going to study math every day and learn long division and fractions," while deep in his heart he had no desire or intention to think about math ever again. The teacher is challenged to help the Jasons set realistic goals and then to meet them, tasks requiring patience, flexibility, and ingenuity.

As in many innovative schools, Clonlara students are neither classified as being in a specific grade group nor given grades as rewards and punishments for the achievements.

Whatever the younger child's avowed goals, students from age five to eight or nine structure their own school activities each day. There is no formal math time or any other time. The teacher observes and only helps a child who shows interest or asks questions. Young Kyla determines her own activities each day, be they intellectual, social, aesthetic, physical, or emotional. Her teacher may provide materials she hopes will stimulate new interests, but the child determines the pace.

The young children always are free to join in the regular classes of their older schoolmates who are required to study math and the language arts. The older students also must participate in the classes they have selected. Thus Clonlara's educational practices diverge from its philosophical ideal of complete child autonomy.

At Clonlara the pace, direction, and content of the curriculum start with the individual student and are determined by combining the skills and concerns of the teachers with the knowledge and aspirations of her or his parents.

Open Classroom Proqram to Bach Open School. From the time of our 1983 visit to the Open Classroom to the 1989 realities of Bach Open School, Ann Arbor's innovative elementary program has functioned with many more curricular restraints than Clonlara.

When the Open Classroom Program first was approved, the teachers were able to jettison the controlled Reading Management System and to teach reading, writing, and thinking together, experientially, to emphasize reading for pleasure and satisfying curiosity. Still they were responsible for covering most of the traditional curriculum. Five of the ten teachers worked during the summer of 1983 on a combined science and social studies curriculum, but for unknown reasons their work was not approved for classroom use. The curricular freedom in the Open School is greater now that it has its own building and principal. Each teacher, however, comes with a long history of independent operation behind closed doors. The school has yet to integrate its operation in a manner similar to the Detroit Open School. The styles of curricular decision making and content vary by teacher.

Most of the open classroom teachers welcome parents warmly, but parental input into curricular planning is limited by the community's political realities. While the individual child remains the philosophical focus of the program, the school board and administrators have more real or potential power than the child, teacher, or parents.

Region Four Open School to Detroit Open School. The similarities between Tomoe School in Tokyo of the 1940s and the Detroit Open School in the 1980s are striking. One could speculate what a conversation between the two school directors would have been like, although getting either away from children would be difficult. The needs of Totto-chan or Rodrigues always would be more immediately important to these school directors than educational abstractions.

Totto-chan's first grade teacher listed the problems and questions in the subjects to be studied that day and told her students to "start with any of these you like." Both independently and with help the young Japanese students tackled all the day's problems and questions.

At Detroit Open School students work in groups and individually. They move as they finish a task or get bored or need help. Hidden at child head level, the teacher is invisible to the casual observer.

"What's happening here?" a third grade boy is asked.

"Everyone knows what to do, and we decide ourselves when to do it," he answers.

"What happens if you don't?"

"You always seem to," he says.

"Always? That's amazing!"

"Well, if you don't want to do something one way, you can always do it another."

"What do you mean? How does that happen?"

"Oh, I don't know," the exasperated nine-year-old says. "Somehow she," and he points at his teacher, "figures out something and it always comes out all right."

At Detroit Open School the students have a sense of purpose balanced with pleasure.

In practice, the Detroit administrators impose little structure on this school, but on paper the demands are greater. To the annoyance of the staff, all students must take the district's standardized achievement tests. With the approval of parents and teachers, enrollment must be 60 percent black and 40 percent other, half boys and half girls. After many successful years and with ardent to militant parent supporters, the staff is free to practice its professionalism together to best fit the needs of the students. Parents are involved in all levels of school operation as active partners with the staff.

When a teacher is asked about the school's curriculum, she relates, "All write journals because we think writing's important. Then we have ideas about where the children are developmentally. Laurajean gives us both freedom and support to do what we think is best. Each year is different, depending on the interests of the kids. I'm doing a lot of short units this year."

"If the teachers have so much freedom and each year's different, how does this school work? How does it all fit together?"

"That's easy. We're all hopelessly curious about what's happening in the whole school. We get together almost every day and talk about what we're trying to do. The school starts with the teachers and students, not the curriculum."

Upland Hills Farm School. The physical environment may be a factor and force in defining and structuring education. At Upland Hills Farm School students inhale knowledge about their environment, from hearing the whir of the windmills generating the school's electricity, to visiting the animals, planting gardens and cooking the produce, to putting an empty juice can in the classroom recycle container. The six paid staff members do most of the teaching, guiding, and planning. The individual child still is the focus, but the contributing forces have changed.

Early mornings usually are spent in small groups working in interrelated ways on writing, reading, math, thinking, and discussing. These groups are formed at the beginning of each year from a base of information, including an informal achievement test. With the exception of final exams for the eighth graders, the students take no other tests.

Each day students of all ages select their activities from a common list. One day these were the choices:

10:30	Rehearsal	12:25	Brent's film
	Outdoor games		Clay
	Clay		Vegetable gardens
	Farm pictures		Jean's music/Ken's
	Wild foods		Compassing

1:15   Rehearsal
          Study time
          Solar cooking
          Compassing

No one obtrusively checks what the students are doing. They come and go, but the teachers are aware of who is where and with whom. Each week's choices are made up in the weekly staff meetings and reflect student interests and teacher skills.

The staff wants all students to grow in confidence, courage and self-understanding. They feel that the content of knowledge is less important than a student's sense of potency and self-esteem, without which content knowledge may be useless.

A boy who has chosen study time asks his teacher if he can work outside.

"Will you be with someone else? Can you work independently?" she asks in return.

"Yes. My self-evaluation says yes. I say yes."

"Alright. But just for me, I'd like to hear from you what happens. Will you let me know?"

"Okay," he says, "I will," and leaves with his work. Self-evaluation is an important part of the curriculum.

Middle and Junior High School

Detroit Open School's middle school program grew out of the elementary program and is six years younger. Not until 1982 did the middle schoolers move in with the elementary children. For many reasons the two programs remain somewhat separate.

The first barrier is that public schools label the middle, junior high, or intermediate schools as secondary schools and their teachers must be certified to teach specific subjects, for example, math, science, social studies, English. Specialist teachers are reluctant to abandon their separateness to work together on integrated learning experiences.

Then, too, the needs of these students are complex and demanding. When Clonlara and Upland Hills had an influx of older students new to this freer, more personally demanding education, they struggled to meet the challenge of adapting to them. The environment in which younger children thrive naturally does not as easily meet the needs of older youth.

These young people who are vacillating between childhood and adulthood no longer are so innocently playful. They need intense interpersonal interaction along with varied intellectual stimulation. If they never have experienced the trust and respect of these innovative schools, they tend to go off halfcocked in sudden freedom to test their limits, sometimes with explosive results.

In her middle school, Laurajean Milligan's first challenge was giving the students some control over their learning lives. One innovation was to require class attendance on certain days and allow free selection of classes on other days. Scheduling was not a difficult problem because students already were assigned to multigrade classes and worked both on individual tasks on their conceptual levels and on group projects. To keep track of attendance, each teacher initialed a student's program card when he or she came to class. The science teacher reports, "There's more learning and excitement for both me and the kids on the voluntary days. If he wants, a student can decide to stay in science or English for two periods one day and skip another."

The next problem was breaking down the barriers between the teachers and their specialized subject matter. Getting the teachers to design interdisciplinary projects was a first step, followed by getting the students involved. Teacher ownership of these interdisciplinary projects was necessary to assure their active participation and commitment.

These teacher/subject matter barriers were insurmountable when the MYA teachers were assigned classrooms far distant from one another. Ann Arbor's restructured intermediate school curriculum also produced knotty scheduling problems which kept seventh and eighth grade students separate. While the four MYA teachers individually structured their own classrooms, they shared a vision of their students setting their own goals and working at their own rates.

The MYA curriculum is broadened by mini-courses which meet four times for an hour a week. One spring mini-course menu included softball with either the social studies or English teacher, silent reading loosely supervised by the science teacher, serious talk led by the science teacher (one day topics included pregnancy, adoptions, marriage, and mothers), and handling stress conducted by a volunteer professional social worker.

Recently, in a more accepting administrative environment and with new staff, the MYA teachers have taken over their own small wing of this large school. The intermediate curriculum will be abandoned entirely in

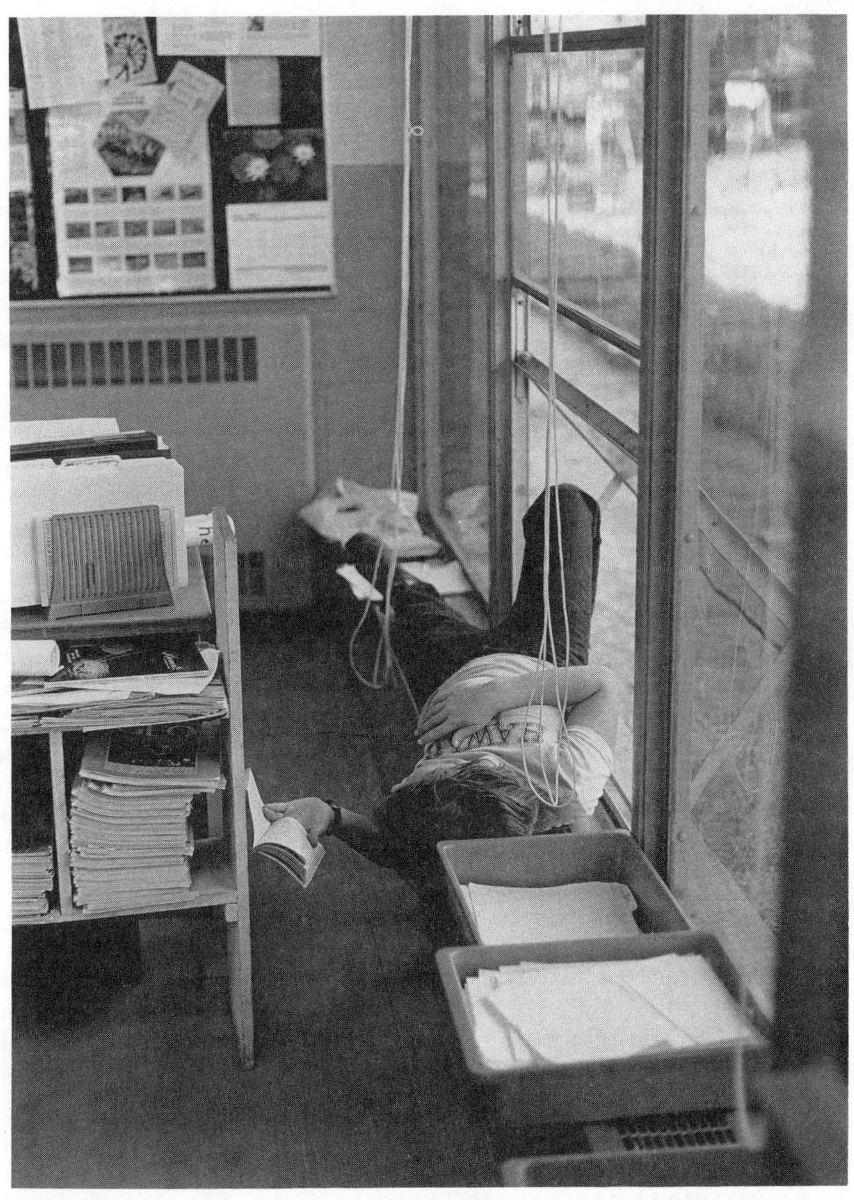

Independent reading in action at Middle Years Alternative. Photograph by
Alex Korn.

1989 when the school system converts to sixth, seventh, and eighth grade middle schools. MYA's future is tenuous as the mainstream program becomes more like MYA's.

Natural Bridge was in a community and state with no desire to control its private schools and consequently the school was blissfully free from watching educational officials. All students were to be learning and advancing in language mastery, social studies, math, and science, but in very nontraditional ways with nontraditional scheduling. In one project, for example, the students who volunteered to collect information on the accessibility of public buildings to people confined to wheelchairs, practiced mathematics, mapmaking, physical education, and more than a little practical social science.

Most students arrived at Natural Bridge convinced that learning only happened in school and that school learning was unavoidably hard and unpleasant. When they found they liked coming to school, they were afraid they could not be learning enough to keep up with their peers in traditional schools. (This common misconception is put to rest in a later chapter.)

Each day began with a group meeting where plans were made, problems aired, and ideas shared. Small skill-based groups, their composition determined by a combination of observation, past performance, standardized achievement tests, and student and teacher desire, met two, three, or five times a week for language arts and math. Students could change groups if they felt they belonged elsewhere. Everyone worked on self-selected individual projects; while Mike struggled to read a book on car racing, Jenny was breeding tropical fish, Tammy was learning about dog training, and David making a survey of comparative religious beliefs. Anyone could request and take any short course in which they were interested; the courses continued as long as students kept coming and expertise could be found. All students had at least one volunteer job in the community. The range of activities was limited only by the imaginations of the students and staff. Parent/student/staff conferences were held at least twice a year and more often if problems warranted, but parental participation in curriculum making was limited by mutual consent. When a boy's mother coerced him into taking French, for example, he consistently sabotaged the class until the staff uncovered his motivation, held a conference, and set him free.

"You can't make me learn," a new student tauntingly announced in group meeting.

"You're absolutely right," a teacher agreed to his dismay. "You're the only one who can do that."

High School

High school builds on the motivation and interests of the middle school years with more highly developed skills and specialized knowledge. High school students need more depth in their learning environments than middle school students, and the learning needs of both differ from elementary children.

Community High is a school of choice, subject to the controls and limitations of the community. To graduate in 1983 Ann Arbor high school students had to acquire twenty units of academic credit properly distributed by subject matter areas. (In times of rising standards, this now has been upped to twenty-two units of credit.) In traditional high schools, students march together through courses in a sequence determined by grade and skill levels. But at Community, subject to teacher approval, students of any age may take any course offered at the school. To encourage experimentation, students can opt for pass/fail instead of letter grades, although in these more conservative times fewer turn down letter grades than before.

Two teachers in the Community Resource Office coordinate student interests with skilled community members. For many years a retired University of Michigan professor taught the required American History course where he shared his living reminiscences of Teddy Roosevelt's presidential campaign. One girl learns automotive mechanics in a gas station, a boy apprentices with a clothing designer, another studies cooking in a restaurant kitchen, while the Community Resource Office assures the academic validity of these community experiences.

Each teacher not only offers courses, but also provides student direction and support as a forum leader. More than a homeroom teacher, the forum leader encourages group discussion, helps organize parties, participates in weekend trips, and more. The boundaries between staff roles are fluid; by student request a secretary, for example, may become a forum leader. The categories of labor which unions thrive upon break down in these innovative schools.

In these schools, the teachers and staff have the strongest overall influence on curriculum. The amount of direct student influence is fairly consistent, but when the community exerts strong control, student input lessens. The physical environment also may contribute to the curriculum in a positive manner (the farm and acres of land at Upland Hills) or in a negative way (the separated rooms at MYA).

CURRICULUM—WHAT DID YOU DO IN SCHOOL TODAY?

All our innovative schools would agree that they want their students to achieve Herbert Kohl's first basic skill, "The ability to use language well and thoughtfully" (Kohl 1982, 110). Traditional schools are sure they are teaching reading when children complete grade appropriate texts and workbooks, but teachers in innovative schools do not equate filling workbook blanks with the ability "to use language well and thoughtfully."

All agree that "reading and writing as basic skills cannot be separated from understanding" (Kohl 1982, 112). The processes by which reading and writing are taught determine the degree and quality of student comprehension as well as the uses to which these skills are put. When the Upland Hills teacher asked a child to evaluate his ability for independent study, her quiet questions taught the boy self-knowledge. Joan Goldsmith and teachers like her strive to understand this "hidden curriculum," i.e. the processes of teaching and relating, to work towards their goals of student self-knowledge, independent thinking, positive self-concept, etc. Instead of, "What did you do in school today?" parents might ask, "How did you do what you did?"

Granted varying degrees of autonomy, these teachers may be able to choose their own methods, curricular content, and activities. Community High students have a smorgasbord of teaching styles from which to get their skills and knowledge. And if they don't like what they see, they can look for approaches more to their liking from others in the community.

Director Laurajean Milligan is the axle about which the wheel of Detroit Open School activities turn. Teachers in the Detroit school system are required to submit complete lesson plans in advance to their principals. The Detroit Open School teachers know it is impossible to predict what they will be doing in the next five minutes, much less next Thursday at 2:00. Their "lesson plans" instead are diaries of ideas, hopes, outcomes, questions, concerns—in short, an exercise in self-exploration. In an ongoing dialogue, Laurajean adds her responses and suggestions to these diaries. Although she constantly is in and out of classrooms, these records are evidence of the validity of the importance of written communication and provide depth to her contacts with the twelve teachers.

After the first two weeks of Natural Bridge, the idea of a curriculum based on individualized, integrated project based programs was shattered. Not only were days too short, and energy too finite for different programs for each student, but this approach failed to take advantage of the social and educational benefits of group interaction. While still important, individual and group projects were joined by ongoing classes, all school events, and many short courses. Most classes met two to three times a week, but the actual schedule was determined in a weekly staff meeting by course content, student need, and teacher availability. At one time there were five math classes with content ranging from place value and long division to geometry and advanced algebra. The students in the middle were drawn to the specialness and secret code words of foreign languages and could choose Spanish, French, and Russian. The staff saw the study of foreign languages as a sneaky way to explore the intricacies of English. During one week, students worked in nine volunteer placements, including an educational television station, the animal shelter, a state hospital, the Junior Museum, and a public elementary school. They could take part in creative dramatics, American history, field trips to the State Senate and to local handbuilt houses, visits to the city and university libraries, music, car mechanics, swimming, Marriage/Independent Living, typing, carpentry, and more. While Natural Bridge students flourished with curricular diversity, courses which the staff thought would be sure-fire successes often failed to catch hold and had to be reconsidered. The freedom to rethink and change unsuccessful plans is all important to innovative schools.

The traditionally educated parent who expects a simple answer to the time honored question, "What did you do in school today?" may be thrown into panic by student answers.

The daily activities vary in these innovative schools, but they share these curricular features:

1. The student is the focal point of the curriculum.
2. The whole child is of curricular concern.
3. Curriculum responds to the developmental needs of the students.
4. The curriculum is flexible.
5. Students participate in determining the pace, content, and order of learning.
6. Learning is interrelated, not broken into small, discrete subject matter categories.

7. Whenever possible, learning is experiential.
8. Curricular goals are complex and future-oriented.

STAFFING—WHO ARE THE TEACHERS?

At the most obvious level, teachers are individuals certified by the state as having met certain standards. Yet in one week, Natural Bridge students had regular contact with two full-time state certified teachers, with a pre-intern education student, with many subject matter experts both out, in, and from the community, with babies, television producers, hospital patients, grandparents, first graders, dogs and cats, and always with one another.

In public schools, all paid teachers must be certified. In Michigan each private school must have at least one appropriately certified teacher, but noncertified people may be hired once the official teacher is in place.

In practice it is nearly impossible to point at all the teachers in an innovative school. Students are teachers when they help one another informally and when they instruct others, their elders included, in how to use a computer or print a photograph. In Japan, at Tomoe School, a farmer taught the children how to grow plants. At Natural Bridge a bank vice-president helped the students set up the Natural Bridge Credit Union.

All teachers in these innovative schools have chosen to be there; they have not been assigned their unique jobs arbitrarily. The best teachers may be those most excited about learning. Enthusiasm is catching, especially from understanding, trusting, honest people.

Whoever they are, teachers in these schools have many parts to play and jobs to do. "More extended and diffuse roles," is how Mary Ann Raywid (1984) described their many functions. Writing an all-inclusive job description is impossible. From helping students with personal problems, to recruiting, cleaning, and fund raising, the work is endless. The successful teacher is enthusiastically committed and spends many waking hours (as well as some sleeping ones) thinking and planning while not actually being with young people.

Raywid found that teachers in alternative public schools are likely to feel they are practicing professionals, free to invent new strategies for reaching individual students. She also noted the "unusual degree of collegiality" we observed in Joan Goldsmith's teacher lounge and lunchroom. Teachers depend more on one another, talk together, share problems and solutions. These observations also apply to our innovative private schools. One test of the quality of daily school life is the pleasure and value the staff takes in talking together. And if they stop talking, trouble has arrived.

The magic number for the "best" student/teacher ratio is impossible to pin down. At Detroit Open School there are thirty-two students to each teacher, as well as many volunteers, and the part-time teacher's aides, who free the staff to lunch together frequently in a nearby restaurant. At Upland Hills in 1983 there were fifty-two students and six teachers, little outside help, and no support personnel.

A private school, dependent on money it raises, never would pay for useless resources, but innovative public schools often receive the same resources as their traditional counterparts, whether they want them or not. Laurajean Milligan pointed at a woman forlornly walking the school corridors and said, "She doesn't have much to do. She's an art teacher, but our teachers integrate art into all their classroom activities."

"The day is so broken up," an Ann Arbor open classroom teacher complained. "The students get started on one thing and have to dash off to art or music or physical education. It doesn't make sense for real learning."

Sometimes private schools can tap into public resources. Clonlara gets help from public school teachers for its students identified as having specific learning difficulties. (Conversely, many parents chose the Detroit Open School because they don't want their children tagged with "learning disabled" labels.) Private schools also may take on different types of activities. Clonlara's burgeoning home schooling program requires consistent secretarial and office help.

The staffs of these innovative schools have the following in common:

1. The proper number of mandated state certified teachers is present, while many others, including students, also teach.
2. The teachers have chosen to work in these schools.
3. The teachers assume many roles and do many different tasks.
4. The teachers are enthusiastic and energetically work long hours; they also get tired.
5. Anyone may be a teacher, anyone a learner.

School Staffing, Chart 3, describes who filled the formal roles in these seven innovative schools in 1983. If no one is identified as taking on a given job, the teachers and students probably were taking it on.

CHART 3
Schoolhouse Staff

Types of Staff/School	Elementary				Intermediate			High
	Clonlara (not preschool)	Upland Hills	Open Classroom	Region Four Open Elementary	Natural Bridge	Middle Years Alternative	Region Four Open Middle	Community High School
Administrator in and out of Classroom	Yes	Yes	No	Yes	Yes	No	Yes	Yes
Paid Teaching Staff Total	4*	6	10	8	3 1/2	4	4	19
Librarian	No	No	Yes	No, Parents Do Job	No, Uses Public Libraries	Yes	No, Parents Do Job	Yes
Learning Disability Teacher	Yes	No (but available)	Yes	Yes	No	Yes	Yes	Yes
Art Music and/or P.E. Teacher	P.E. (Y.M.C.A.)	No	Yes	Yes	Yes	Yes	Yes	Yes

Aides	No	No	Yes	Yes	No	No	Yes	Yes
Volunteers	Yes	Yes	Yes	Yes	Yes	Yes	Yes	Yes
Office/Clerical Paid	Yes	No	Yes	Yes	No	Yes	Yes	Yes
Janitor/ Cleaning Paid	Yes**	Yes***	Yes	Yes	No	Yes	Yes	Yes
Transportation to and from School	Yes	Teachers Take Turns	Yes	Yes	No	Yes	Yes	Yes
Counselor****	No	No	No	No	No	No	No	Yes
School Psychologist	Sometimes Available	No	Yes	Sometimes Available	No	Yes	Yes	Yes

*Including unpaid Pat Montgomery.
**Parents work as part of tuition payment.
***Twice a week.
****Teachers assume role of counselors in all schools.

Teacher Selection

Who chooses the teachers? The exact procedures vary both from school to school and from hiring to hiring, but students, parents, and staff all may have a say.

"Teachers in schools of choice need to be both generalists and specialists to a degree which many teachers currently are not," Mary Anne Raywid explained in a speech to the National Commission of Excellence in Teacher Education (1984, 7). Finding teachers is not simple.

At Clonlara many paid teachers started as volunteers. They had sought out the school, knew the program, and were known by everyone, but this is not a common solution to teacher selection.

More often teachers are chosen by how well they perform in interviews. But despite everyone's best efforts, warm, compassionate interview behavior may have little relationship to actual classroom behavior. Nor does talking with parents, teachers, and students necessarily let the teacher know what he or she is in for.

The Clonlara parent/student/staff board, a group comprised of any willing volunteers from these three categories, hires teachers for the school. Recently five parents, three staff members, and four students sifted through applications from sixty people who said they wanted to teach the older, grade five and up, students. During the summer the board reduced the number of applicants first to twelve, then to the final four who would be interviewed.

How much teaching have you done? What do you know about Clonlara? What have you read? What have you done in nontraditional schools? What are your strong points? Your weak points? One candidate at first fielded questions with aplomb. A student asked if he'd take the students "to the parks and that river you just talked about."

"If it's possible," answered the candidate.

"Well then," a parent zeroed in, "what would you do if it was time to leave and one of the children didn't want to come?"

"I'd say he had to come. When I tell a kid to do something, I expect to be obeyed. I'd pick him up and put him in the car if I had to," the unsuccessful candidate explained. Blind obedience is not a Clonlara goal.

Many interviews later the board agreed unanimously on a teacher with twenty-five years experience, an explanation for taking such a low paying job, and an understanding answer to the question, "What would you do if a child spit in your beard?" After experiencing the realities of this form of nontraditional education for six weeks, this newly hired teacher decided to quit teaching at Clonlara and go back to school. The board went back to work, but that's another tale.

At Upland Hills a teacher applicant spends at least two days in the school interacting with the staff and students. The school's board of directors, composed of parents and other community members, allows Phil Moore to hire staff, but he shares this responsibility with the other teachers, always taking student opinion into account.

No Natural Bridge teacher was hired without being seen in action. The first two were observed in a traditional public school classroom and during a tutoring session, but as soon as there were Natural Bridge students, applicants came to school to share their interests and skills. The students often saw characteristics their elders overlooked. After a skilled science teacher had kept students engrossed an entire afternoon with science mysteries, Tammy said he was okay but nothing special. "It's like, well, he was afraid or something."

Jenny said more pointedly, "There's something kind of weak about him," and he confirmed her view by simply disappearing without further notice.

Teachers may be attracted to innovative schools for the wrong reasons. Some equate the freedom to make decisions with freedom from responsibility.

Ideally the teacher is a member of an educational team, one which strengthens the team as a whole. Selection is demanding both for the applicant and the school.

When the lure of greater authority and autonomy drew a successful MYA math teacher to a traditional college preparatory school, the search for his replacement was on. Throughout a long, hot summer a constantly changing self-selected committee of parents, students, teachers, and community members interviewed and argued cantankerously over candidates. In July everyone agreed on the perfect candidate, only to be told by the district personnel office, which had provided the application, that he was not qualified for the job. Although he was to teach seventh and eighth grade math, he was not sufficiently educated to teach twelfth grade advanced placement math courses, and, who knew, what with declining enrollment and all, he might be required to do just that. The details differed, but the outcome was the same a dozen interviews later when a hard-won agreement was reached again. Twenty-three candidates later, the students felt betrayed by their elders, the parents were feuding, and a teacher who would have been rejected twenty-one interviews before was offered the job. Open-ended participation in teacher

CHART 4
Who Chooses Teachers

School	Students	Parents	Staff	Building Administrator	Others (community)	Decision Process	Final Authority
Clonlara	Yes Committee Representative	Yes Committee	Yes Committee	Yes Committee	—	Concensus	Parent/Staff Student Committee
Upland Hills Farm School	Yes Advisory Power	—	Yes	Yes	—	Mutual Agreement	School Director Hired by Board of Directors
Natural Bridge	Yes Advisory Power	Opinions Sought	Yes	Yes	Opinions Sought	Mutual Agreement	Director

Open Classroom Program	No	Yes Committee Advisory	Yes Committee Advisory	Yes	Central Admin- istration	Agreement, Sometimes Mutual	District Personnel Office
Region Four Open School	No	Yes Hiring Committee	Yes Hiring Committee	Yes Committee	—	Mutual Agreement	District Personnel Office
Middle Years Alternative	Yes Committee	Yes Committee	Yes Committee (if they desired)	Yes	Yes Committee	Mutual Agreement	Principal plus District Personnel Office
Community High School	Yes Committee	Yes Committee	Yes Committee	Yes Committee	Yes Committee	Caucus Vote	District Personnel Office

selection may be chaotic; MYA now has a more organized procedure.

Parents have a hard-won voice in teacher selection in the Ann Arbor Open Classroom Program and Bach Open School. Community High's ideal interviewing procedure assures that the voices of parents, teachers, support staff, students, and community members will be heard. For many years the spirit of anti-authoritarianism disenfranchised the Community High dean from participating in staff selection, although influence might be exerted in other ways. Whatever a committee's conclusions, in these public schools the final hiring decision rests with the district's personnel office.

Detroit Open School's hiring committee consists of parents, teachers, and a procedure. Sung to the tune of "I'm Looking Over a Four-Leaf Clover" by parents and teachers at their tenth anniversary party these lyrics tell their story:

> We're looking over some prospective teachers
> That we haven't seen before.
> Some of them fancy
> And some of them plain,
> Some full of ideas that give us a pain.
> We ask them questions
> Then we listen
> To see what they have to say.
> It can be confusing to do the choosing
> For teaching the Open School way.

The participants in staff hiring in the seven settings are illustrated in Chart 4.

Teacher hiring is an area of school decision making in which many constituencies participate. Teaching in an innovative school is so complex that selected candidates may withdraw or fail under fire. Shared responsibility, shared governance, is a goal of these alternative, open schools, but students, especially public elementary school students, have less voice in the processes and content of their curricular activities than their elders.

Chapter 6

More Common Ground

Ideally governance in these innovative schools includes everyone. Realistically the potential for input from different constituencies depends on the nature of issue—from "What will I do today?" questions, goal definition, appropriate teaching methods, teacher selection, to allocating never enough dollars. The deadlines for important decisions always come too soon. Who plays a part in governance partially is determined by the peculiar nature of the crisis at hand and the time frame for action.

Long-lived innovative schools have found a balance between the pressures of daily life and their ideals. Without faith in the validity of their goals and without respect for others, achieving this balance point would be impossible.

Yet in one area of educational life there are no compromises.

Relationships

"Now then, tell me all about yourself," Sosaku Kobayashi asked the little girl seated next to him. Japanese television star Tetsuko Kuroyanagi reported that never before had she, Totto-chan, met someone who listened so long and so well. For the first time in her seven years she was with an adult, not a parent, not a relative, whom she really liked. And wonder of wonders, this person was the headmaster of a school.

The respect, trust, and friendship between this school director and a little girl exemplify the most important quality of our innovative schools. While their activities may differ, their goals lean one way or another, their resources vary, they are united in the quality of their interpersonal relationships.

Most teachers in traditional schools like children. Otherwise they would not be following their difficult profession. Many teachers feel their job is to hand down their own knowledge to their students whose role it is to accept and master that which their teachers give. Teacher satisfaction comes from the smooth flow of this one-way stream. For the good of the student the teacher is empowered to do almost anything to assure the one-way current is not blocked.

Totto-chan was expelled from her traditional school because she thought education went two ways. She was enchanted by the street musicians who played outside her school window and tried to bring them to her teacher's attention. When the horrified teacher ignored her, the little girl talked with the musicians, thereby ending this phase of her education.

The traditional teacher has almost unlimited power over his or her students. It is true that many excellent traditional teachers bypass this power trip and establish comfortable two-way relations with their students whom they both like and respect. But in traditional schools such interaction between teachers and students may be more the exception than the rule.

Our innovative schools are characterized by warm, respectful human interactions. The younger people learn from their elders—and the elders learn from their juniors. By virtue of having lived and learned longer, the elders have more knowledge and experience, but the younger students bring their own perceptions and creativity, their unique experience and knowledge to these schools. Respect for teachers is neither legislated nor mandated but grows naturally from shared experience.

Once upon a time, the Natural Bridge teachers thought a quick assessment of student computational skills would be useful. Perhaps the teachers needed reassurance that students were learning. Perhaps it was time to form new skill groups. The rationale for the test has been forgotten, but not the lessons it taught. Anticipating student resistance, the teachers decided they would be guinea pigs and try their quiz first on themselves. Suddenly they found themselves tense and anxious, then realized the students would have the same feelings. When the teachers corrected their tests (just as the students would), they all had made mistakes and, by reflex, found excuses for their errors. The next day they told their juniors what had transpired, then explained seriously that their small and insignificant failures were caused by smeared ink and haste, not ignorance. The implication was that student mistakes were genuine errors, but teacher mistakes should be forgiven. The students howled with laughter when they heard their own righteous excuses coming out of teacher mouths. With full knowledge of their teachers' fallibility, they took the little quiz—and the few who did better than any elder chortled with glee. The teachers not only had a lesson in humility, but also gained student respect for demonstrating their faults so vividly. Honesty is more powerful than false perfection.

At Clonlara the ideal teacher/student relationship is one of equality. When the MYA students were asked what made their program different, Josh explained that it was the teachers. "They're more like friends," he said.

"Most of the teachers care about you," Cindy added, "but there's one I'd better not say anything more about." Given the chance, young people are painfully honest about their feelings, and teachers in these schools understand and respect their candor.

Talking about honesty and respect is easier than living them minute by minute. In reality teachers get tired and cranky, but when one is fed up with a certain student, that student can get guidance and support from another teacher for a time. Open classroom children in both Ann Arbor and Detroit are able to visit other rooms and teachers just as their teachers are able to find ways to shift responsibility for a given child.

The many shapes and functions of evaluation flow from the well-spring of supportive, trusting interpersonal relationships.

EVALUATION

"How can you tell what you've learned if you don't get grades?" a fifth grader asked on his first visit to Clonlara.

"What about asking yourself? You probably know better than any-one."

"Not me," he said in disbelief. "I'm not smart enough to know what I've learned."

The staffs of our innovative schools would disagree unanimously with John. Who better to know about learning than the learner? Evaluation simply is one incident of many in the ongoing process of learning. Never the endpoint, evaluation helps define what happens next.

Most participants in the idealistic revolutionary schools of the 60s and 70s thought evaluation was a dirty word. For many reasons they held a deep "ideological and emotional prejudice against anything that smacks of objective evaluation and judgment" (Graubard 1972, 152). Nevertheless, the students, parents, and teachers in these schools argued, reviewed the past and planned for the future during many marathon talk sessions. These discussions, often heated, actually were a kind of living program evaluation, but the participants' deep fear of arbitrary authoritarianism kept them from recording and formalizing their judgments.

The following purposes of evaluation are as vital and useful today as when formulated nearly a half century ago by participants in the Eight-Year Study. None are "traditional" in the sense of ranking students by academic worthiness.

1. Evaluation provides the means for assessing effectiveness of a particular educational institution, to determine what is working well and where changes are required.
2. Appropriate evaluation may "validate the hypotheses upon which the educational program operates." If it is found, for example, that children who are respected and allowed to follow their own interests actually do become self-motivated learners, important implications follow for educational institutions in general. (Evidence concerning this particular hypothesis follows in the next chapter.)
3. Evaluation may provide students with information to help them make better educational and career decisions. On the other hand, whenever tests and grades are used primarily to exclude students from educational and career possibilities, to close off their options, "evaluation" results in narrow, poor decisions.
4. Well-executed evaluation may provide a sense of psychological security to students, their parents, and the school staff. Days flow by so rapidly that pausing to assess progress may contribute to everyone's psychological wellbeing.
5. Evaluation may provide the basis for the positive public relations which allow these controversial innovative schools to exist (Smith, Tyler, et al. 1942).

Long-lived alternative schools are characterized by continual evaluation and modification (Case 1981). Our innovative schools always have to face up to the successes and failures of their students. How has Kate changed this year? What skills has Nicky developed? How does he use them? Less often do these schools have the luxury of stepping back and comprehensively evaluating the effectiveness of their total learning program. Community High School is an exception in that it undergoes periodic institutional scrutiny to maintain its accreditation from the North Central Association of Colleges and Schools.

Report card grades and test scores traditionally rank a student against his or her peers. Many parents are satisfied that these letters and numbers accurately describe their children, but such evaluation is narrow at best and can be destructive at worst.

If our alternative schools do employ tests, they are used as tools to assist learning. Our school staffs diverge sharply from traditional educators on this point. They act on the belief that human potentials are too many and too varied to be summarized even by a battery of test scores.

Weaning students from the props of grades and moving them towards taking responsibility for their own learning is, to say the least, challenging. After three report cardfree years, probably in anticipation of the cruel, cold world of public high school, a few Natural Bridge students led a revolt for letter grades instead of verbal descriptions of actual achievements. The staff responded with an interim form on which students rated their degree of involvement in different activities and gave themselves their own grades for performance. In meetings, the students compared the grades they gave themselves with those assigned by teachers. Teachers and students together argued about discrepancies, and ultimately reached two-way compromises. This one-time exercise in grading both cleared the air and allowed everyone to learn.

Evaluation is an interactive process in which teachers and students share. When left to judge themselves on their own, students can be harsh and uncompromising. Jessie, for one, consistently degraded and bad-mouthed herself, probably so others couldn't say worse about her, thereby maintaining control of what she had come to see as a bad situation. Helping her come to terms with her many virtues and talents, to grow in positive self-knowledge, was barely begun when her family moved to another city, but a few seeds had been planted. Teachers can provide the perspective which increases student objectivity.

Classroom tests and grades are live, controversial issues in Ann Arbor's open classrooms. Because the elementary teachers have come together after years in their isolated and often besieged classrooms, each has confidence in the validity of his or her own beliefs and practices. Whatever lip service is given to a unifying philosophy, classroom practices differ profoundly. One teacher complains bitterly that her colleague, who persists in giving tests and letter grades, is destroying the fragile confidence she had worked so hard to build in her former students. The grade-giving teacher demeans her colleague's charges and claims that she is building confidence by preparing her students for the cruel world of junior high school. Both feel they are acting in the best interests of children.

Whatever the niceties of philosophical premises, standardized tests, such as the norm based California Achievement Tests (CAT) and the reference based Michigan Tests of Educational Progress (MEAP), are mandatory in our innovative public schools. Most teachers have not yet resolved their ambivalence about the significance of their students' test performances. On one hand, deep in their hearts they understand that test scores are unrelated to what they are trying to accomplish. They know that students develop in irregular fits and starts, each at a different rate; they recognize that Jimmy's scores were affected both by his persistent cold and his pet turtle's recent death. Yet they are haunted by a lingering fear that low scores are the embodiment of their personal failure as teachers. Perhaps they should be doing more. "What I really need," Joan Goldsmith said, "is someone to reassure me from time to time. To tell me it's okay if Mark isn't reading yet and he's starting the third grade, to say I can give him more time." With neither grades nor test scores as artificial props, these teachers are accustomed to bouts of middle-of-the-night worrying .

Upland Hills refuses to subject their children to standardized tests, but recently Clonlara students insisted they wanted to take the CAT so they could be just like their public school friends. Possibly they were looking for reassurance about how they measured up in the world outside Clonlara.

In spite of moral and ethical objections raised by the students, Natural Bridgers were subjected to the Sequential Tests of Educational Progress (STEP) at regular intervals. While their arguments about the validity of tests had educational value, the misery-making tests were given so that a) students would learn how to handle themselves in test situations, b) the tests would lose their mystical powers, c) the information could be used in curricular planning, and d) to provide evidence respected by the outside world that Natural Bridge's strange and irregular practices resulted in gains on whatever tests measure.

Evaluation must be continuous. At the end of each day Upland Hills students return to their home groups to talk about what they have done and how they feel about their accomplishments. Doris Sperling's students record their activities each day and rate the quality of their per-

Students evaluate their day at Upland Hills Farm School. Photograph by Alex Korn.

formances on many different criteria. Each night at home the teacher responds to her students' daily self-evaluations.

Most of these innovative teachers have some method for recording student descriptions and activities. The time and energy available for ongoing record keeping is always in short supply, however, so they change frequently. Teacher-written narrative accounts, often with student self-evaluations, provide the basis for periodic conferences and reports to students and parents.

Only Clonlara keeps no written records of a child's work. This school's rationale is that each year every child deserves a completely fresh start.

What letter grade can equal this thirteen-year-old's language arts evaluation? "You are much more able to express yourself in complete sentences and your creative writing is flowing more freely," the teacher wrote. "You seem to be more comfortable at putting your feelings in words. Your most complex thoughts still may show up as sentence fragments, but your thinking is good and the problem only mechanical. Even your penmanship is improving, as is your typing. You have mastered the steps of composition and your neat final paper for the composition unit was beautiful. Your spelling is more accurate, too. You are taking responsibility for your work!" Is this a B? Perhaps a C+? Why not an A-?

MYA and Community High assign traditional letter grades for coursework; usually these grades are given on the basis of contracts drawn up at the beginning of a semester between student and teacher (and at MYA parents are included). Grades do not drop arbitrarily from the sky but are based on mutually understood expectations. Community also may give pass/fail grades, but unfortunately colleges seldom know what to do with them.

Eighth graders at Detroit Open School are assigned secret, "hidden" grades which may be unveiled if, for example, a magnet high school insists on knowing the "calibre" of the applying student. Any dispute between a teacher and the school director about what grade to assign is resolved by giving the higher one. "We all live up to the expectations people have for us, don't we?" Laurajean Milligan says.

Ann Arbor's open classrooms had to use the same non-letter grade reporting forms as their traditional colleagues but the teachers always added more to their reports. (Bach Open School now has devised its own evolving evaluation procedures.) While her students play outside, Lovey Bradley stares at page after page of computer-printed numbers. "I've got to look at these before I write reports to my parents. They'll get copies of the test scores," she explains. "Most of my kids did really well on the first test they had to take in the fall, and a lot of people don't seem to realize that if you score at the top of a test, you're not likely to improve when you take it again. I hate this," she says and jams the sheets back into a cupboard.

The innovative elementary schools hold frequent parent/student/teacher conferences. While parents and teachers are accustomed to talking together, many students have a primitive fear of being outnumbered by adults. Realizing that youth and age are on the same team is an important discovery. Every MYA student has at least two of these meetings each year, in time carved out of a traditional intermediate school schedule. Community High is the only school of our seven which does not schedule regular parent/student/teacher conferences.

Other innovative schools have developed sophisticated evaluation methods. Prospect School, a long-lived private school for four and one-half to thirteen-year-olds in North Bennington, Connecticut, has developed a process to evaluate student development which also may be applied to the curriculum, a particular issue, a teaching practice, a class, or an entire school. At Prospect, teachers systematically record narrative descriptions of their students and collect samples of their work. Student evaluation includes a systematic, open, and responsive interview process through which a whole child's developmental progress is integrated and illuminated. The Prospect Archives hold samples of children's work collected over time. By studying children's drawings, writing, and other recordable productions (their work has been stripped of personal identifying markers), researchers may follow the progress and development of real children as they live their rich, complex lives. The Prospect Archives hold a wealth of information through which "the mesh of schools curriculum, structures, and teaching practice with the individual learning and thinking modes of children" may be explored (Carini 1982, 4).

For high school graduation the St. Paul Open School requires documented competence instead of grades from coursework. St. Paul Open School students participate actively in their educations as they collect proof of their competence in information finding, career awareness, personal-interpersonal skills and communication, consumer awareness, cultural awareness, community involvement, and current issues (Nathan 1983).

Risk taking is part of learning, and some educational outcomes are bound to be less successful or satisfying than others. All our schools would insist that students have the right to make mistakes. Yet teachers often resist or are unable to apply this right to their own lives. A few years after quitting both Natural Bridge and the teaching profession, a former teacher returned to the empty schoolhouse on a late afternoon, then recorded his reactions in a letter. "Looking back on that hour alone I was surprised some of my best moments at Natural Bridge School were when I was failing. Natural Bridge allowed time for failing, for discovering that failure is not that big of a deal. I believed it for the kids but not for myself." Learning is life long.

To summarize, evaluation:

1. is part of the learning process.
2. may include testing to aid learning, not to categorize children.
3. is interactive and includes input from everyone involved in the learning process.
4. is continual.
5. should be applied to teachers, students, the learning process, the curriculum, the school.

School Size

Our alternative open schools are small; the seven we have seen enrolled from thirty to four hundred students at the time of our visit. The special teacher/student relationships would not thrive in big, impersonal institutions. Because some schools are larger than others it may be more accurate to say that these alternative schools are structured to act and feel small. Always there is a sense of belonging, a feeling of shared responsibility.

John Goodlad sent trained observers into more than a thousand classrooms in thirty-eight different schools where they discovered that the most satisfied students, teachers, and parents tended to be in small schools. Goodlad proposed that large schools should reorganize themselves into smaller units by breaking up vertically, across the grade levels. Meaningful teacher/student contacts would increase in these smaller mixed-age and grade schools within large school buildings and student alienation decrease. A powerful sense of belonging would grow from being with a stable group of teachers and fellows over time (Goodlad 1984).

Researchers studying traditional urban and rural high schools found that students in small schools were more satisfied and participated more in school activities than those in large schools. Academically marginal students, in particular, experienced school life differently within big and small institutions. Borderline students in big schools felt they were outsiders, but borderline students in schools small enough to need every student to carry out voluntary school activities were active, needed participants (Barker and Cump 1964).

The typical alternative secondary program in 1980 enrolled fewer than two hundred students; only a handful actually had more (Raywid 1980). Hofstra University's Center for the Study of Educational Alternatives goes so far as to advise schools and programs to stay small for survival. "Most successful programs are at some point or other tempted to enlarge," their tip sheet reads. "It's flattering and enticing, but don't succumb to overexpansion or the lure of empire building. Smallness is an important part of what you've got going for you."

PARENTS AND THEIR CHILDREN

Who would send their children to these schools? And why?

"People don't always choose us because they want an open school," Laurajean Milligan states candidly. "They have lots of different reasons. Some have heard it's a good school. Others think their children will get more individual attention, but they don't understand our philosophy at all. We have all kinds of parents and all kinds of kids."

The single characteristic all the parents have in common is that they have made a choice about their children's educations; they have taken action instead of passively accepting whatever traditional program comes their way. Before their admission procedures were altered to make them less blatantly visible, Detroit Open School applicants may have had to wait in a line day and night for a week or more. (Television crews found the scene irresistible and hopeful parents might find themselves on the nightly news—to the annoyance of some public school officials.) As for the private schools, parents not only search them out but also are willing to pay for them. Their efforts may be amply rewarded. "For the first time my son wants to go to school," a father reported. "Even when we're early, David tells me to drive faster so he won't miss anything."

Many of the Upland Hills and Natural Bridge parents were and are professional educators employed by public education. Some had to struggle painfully with their consciences to make the decision to send their children to a private school.

As a rule the parents of children in these alternative schools are neither wealthy nor powerful, but represent all walks of life. At Clonlara the parents of 35 percent of the children, especially preschoolers, are unable to pay tuition and work at the school in return for tuition credits. The private schools, on principle, reduce tuition to fit a parent's income.

These schools want children from all parts of society in their educational microcosms. Admission is open to all, provided space is available. To maintain its gender and racial balance, the Detroit Open School fills vacancies (only six in a typical year other than new kindergartners) with the first on the waiting list who matches the departed student in grade, sex, and race.

In Ann Arbor persistent and sometimes contradictory stereotypes flourish about the students in alternative education. The elementary school parents are accused of isolating themselves from racial diversity as they create an educational program fine tuned for their academically talented, white wunderkind. At the intermediate level the students are perceived as weaklings unable to cope with the rigorous intellectual and social demands of traditional intermediate school. And Community High students are seen as deviants, undesirables, and drug-using academic losers.

In a community where 17 percent of the elementary students are black, 10 percent of the Open Classroom Program children were black as were two of their ten teachers; 8 percent of the students were members of other minority groups.

A number of parents are attracted to the individualized program at the Detroit Open School because they don't want their children to be stigmatized by being labelled "learning disabled." One of the sites of the Open Classroom Program had a higher percent (7 percent) of identified learning disabled than the traditional program with which it shared a building (5.8 percent). On a survey constructed and administered by school system officials, many Open Classroom parents reported that their children's special academic needs were being met by open education. A mother whose son had difficulty learning to read noted on her form, "I am grateful to the OCP because with all his problems he loves school. He is repeating the fourth grade and in OCP that is not a stigma. In a traditional program he would have flunked."

Student achievement will be addressed in a more leisurely fashion further on, although no explanation will be offered as to why many people prefer myths to facts.

Sometimes parents do select these schools for the wrong reasons.

A girl came to Natural Bridge because, for whatever reasons, her mother wanted her to skip a grade by doing two years work in one. The student certainly wanted to leap ahead in grade placement, but work was not part of her plan. Together the girl, her mother, and the staff developed a contract with well-defined standards to demonstrate competence, but the student, often with maternal support, was a masterful manipulator. Conferences expanded to include grandparents, but no comfortable resolutions were found all the frustrating years she stayed in the school.

Parents who are sympathetic to the school's philosophy and goals may object when they see the practices required to reach those goals. "Why hasn't Mark learned his multiplication tables?" the Clonlara parent asks.

"He hasn't decided he's ready yet," his teacher answers. "He's busy with other work."

"That doesn't look like work to me," the mother says with disgust as she watches her eight-year-old build a block road system with a small friend. "Are you going to let him play all day?"

If Mark's or another child's parents are sufficiently upset, they may try to change the school's practices, and that has happened in both our private and public schools. A school with a secure staff united in philosophy and goals will not be threatened by a dissenting parent, but woe is sure to visit the wishy-washy. Perhaps the staff will be able to work with the child and parents to change practices in an imaginative and creative fashion acceptable to all. Or the parent, with child attached, may decide to leave the school. These are schools of choice.

Older students may have to exert pressure to get parental permission to attend the school of their choice. Community High's reputation alarms some adults. Students over sixteen who decide Community is for them simply may threaten to drop out of school if they don't get their way. Younger high schoolers may encourage their parents to visit the school, and talk with teachers and veteran Community parents. Yet a parent could see the individualistically costumed CHS students, be terrified by a girl with green and orange hair, and not even hear the terrifying punk ask politely if the parent needs help.

The students in our schools come from many backgrounds; they have wildly diverse skills, interests, and abilities. Students are challenged to learn how to make choices and decisions by doing, and making mistakes. Sometimes they have to unlearn what other schools taught them. With time and practice they learn to ask questions, to trust themselves and others, and to find the courage to look for answers.

DISCIPLINE

Discipline is a major problem in traditional schools, but ask one of our alternative school teachers how he or she maintains discipline. First the teacher looks puzzled and thinks hard. Then you may be asked to repeat the question, for in these schools discipline is not a commodity maintained by an outside authority. Both the educational atmosphere and staff practices encourage the growth of discipline from within each student. Maladaptive actions and misdeeds—especially those which hurt others—do have consequences, but consequences which help the student learn and grow. Punishments are not invoked for the sole purpose of temporary behavioral control.

A.S. Neill has said that adults have an unfortunate tendency to substitute discipline for understanding the child. Important educational goals at Clonlara are that children live with others and to take responsibility for their own actions. At age seven, Matthew is in constant motion and never stops long enough to see how much he annoys others. When six-year-old Sara couldn't stand his actions any longer, she called a meeting. Before she rang the summoning bell, she had tried her six-year-old best to reason with Matthew, but he'd persisted in knocking over her blocks. Now Sara was mad.

Clonlara students, age five to sixteen sat in a circle and heard Sara's side. "Matthew is always getting in my way. He dumped my blocks after I told him to stop. He laughed at me!"

"Sara had all of them," Matthew answered back. "I took a red block 'cuz I needed it. She looks funny when she's mad." Matthew laughed some more.

"It's not funny! How do you like it when someone laughs at you, Matthew?" fifteen-year-old Liz asked.

"I don't care," he answered too quickly, then added, "I don't like it."

"I think I know how he feels. I used to be like that," Jason, twelve, said. "I got in everyone's way because I wanted someone to notice me. No one liked me, but I got lots of attention."

"Maybe we need to pay attention to him before he gets in trouble. What do you think, Matthew?" Matthew said he felt pretty good when people paid attention to him.

"Let's try it," Liz said. "We could take turns." The students worked out a schedule so Matthew would get the attention he craved while he learned to be more aware of his own behavior. Only with child help

Hands-on problem resolution at Clonlara. Photograph by Alex Korn.

would adults have come up with such an ingenious solution.

Open classroom teachers provide discipline by sitting on the floor with their children and helping them learn to solve their own social problems.

Only two rules were imposed on Natural Bridge students at the beginning of the first year. They were not to destroy one another and they were to be respectful of the school's wary neighbors. The first day a third was added; unless given permission, no student was to dance, write, walk, sit, or do anything on the brittle roof of the three-story building—and the reason was that we had no money available for roof repair. New rules were added by the students and staff together to solve new problems. One year any student making a nuisance by running in the house was required, when requested by anyone, to run around the outside of the building three times—rain or steamy heat. Each year all rules but the first three were discarded to give everyone a fresh start.

Discipline policy in traditional schools usually is set by adults who do not take part in daily school life. Although exclusion from school for being late or playing hooky would appear to reward the misbehavior, many institutions do just that. A seventh grader came to Natural Bridge after being suspended for two weeks from his traditional school. This punishment was to teach him not to walk out of classes where he claimed he was wasting his own and the teacher's time. In a new setting gradually he let down his guard and admitted he couldn't read well enough to understand the textbooks and worksheets in his former school and, indeed, was wasting his own and his teacher's time by going to class.

Students like coming to these alternative schools. They do not want to be suspended or sent home. Whenever we tried to send Natural Bridge students home for a half day of teacher planning, they refused to be evicted and even crawled through windows to return. Future nonstudent planning times were held in a staff member's home. (Perhaps the students were saying that staff privacy was against school philosophy; whatever the statement, the staff badly needed time away from students to stop and plan.) Detroit Open School resorted to exclusion only once. An angry middle school student new to the program found her life crumbling around her: Charlene's father had left home, her mother was sick, her beloved grandfather was dying, the family had no money, and the problems would not stop. Again and again the girl picked fights at school; she stole small items and cash and refused help from others. After broken promises and incidents had piled up, in a fit of anger Laurajean Milligan suspended the girl—for three days. After suffering through a tormented sleepless night, the director allowed the tearful, repentant girl to return the next day. Charlene got along a little better after her shortened expulsion, but nothing magical transpired. Her teachers continued to lavish her with support and encouragement—just as they do all their students.

At Detroit Open School parents are called in at the first signs of problems, not to enact punishments but to be a member of the parent/student/staff team.

Crises are not scheduled in advance. A Japanese television crew was filming Clonlara school life when an older boy, not unlike Charlene, required immediate attention. Student solutions had failed. The boy, his parents, and teacher met in Pat Montgomery's office while a newspaper reporter and the video team observed a teacherless class working on their math. This student also was suspended against his wishes; he didn't want to leave, but he needed time to understand the consequences of his disruptive behavior.

Staff roles change constantly. While their jobs defy easy definition, they are not enforcers of discipline. They are partners in creating an atmosphere in which self-discipline will grow.

RESOURCES

While talking about what these schools are not, physical environment has to be mentioned. These schools are not neat and tidy. They tend to look run down. They flourish in unusual places and buildings rejected by others. They have neither swimming pools nor groomed, blacktop playgrounds. A number of reasons account for their decrepit exteriors.

The most important reason is that their precious financial resources are spent on people, on teachers, not on buildings and materials. Community High's elementary school-sized auditorium is too small to house high school graduation ceremonies, so a beautiful church across the street lends its facilities to the students for important occasions.

These schools do not have to own physical resources; they only need to get access to them. Clonlara looks shabby but Clonlara students use the first rate gymnasium and swimming pool at the Ann Arbor Y. One of Clonlara's ancient portable classrooms contains a sizeable library, but students make frequent trips to the city library. Movie projectors, films, and other equipment may be borrowed. Upland Hills students do not need elaborate laboratories while they learn biology, and plant growth by growing plants. The carcass of an old car hidden in a fold in the hills provides a lab for beginning physics and automobile mechanics.

CHART 5
School Resources

School	Clonlara	Upland Hills Farm School	Natural Bridge	Open Classroom	Region Four Open	Middle Years Alternative	Community High
Shared Building	No	No	No	Yes	Yes	Yes	No
Sports Facilities	Uses Y.M.C.A. Outdoor Space	Acres of Outdoors	Y.M.C.A. and Two Public Parks	School Gym and Fields	School Gym	Gym, Tennis, Swimming, Fields	Tiny Gym
Auditorium Stage	No	No Uses Dome	No Used Large Room	Yes	Yes	Yes	Small Auditorium
Library	Yes	Many Books in Rooms	Limited, Used Public Libraries	Yes	Yes Parent Run	Yes	Yes

Film Projectors, etc.	Borrows	Yes	Borrowed	Yes	Yes	Yes	Yes
Computer	Yes	Yes	Borrowed	Yes	No	Yes	Yes
Video	No	No	Yes	Yes	No	Yes	Yes
Movie, Cameras, etc.	No	No	Yes	Yes	No	May Borrow	Yes
Science Lab Equipment	No	Some	Some	Some	Some	Yes	Yes

Note: Access to equipment does not mean equipment is utilized.

It is the human resources who stretch their minds to find necessary physical resources.

All of these innovative schools have access to at least one computer. Parents at Detroit Open School have supplied a computer room.

All schools except Clonlara maintain miniature zoos, although Community's zoo consists mainly of scheduled animals in the science rooms and unscheduled visiting dogs and boa constrictors accompanied by their owners.

Real learning is not neat and compartmentalized; in these schools learning overflows boundaries. "My room's a mess, isn't it?" observes a Detroit Open School teacher. "There never seems to be anything I can do about it." Book stacks teeter on tables. Project leftovers balance on tall bookcases. Blackboards are hidden behind piles of learning possibilities. A new student-made pioneer sodhouse made from living green grass holds a place of honor alone on a table.

Busy students do not notice the clutter, although they complain when they can't find needed materials.

At the end of the Upland Hills school day, five-year-old Marla spontaneously picks up anything dropped on the floor. A tiny boy wipes the blackboard clean with a wet sponge. When asked what she's doing, Marla explains that it's her job.

"How did you get this job?"

"Look here," she says, pointing at a list of tasks matched with student names. "That's how we know what to do."

Adult custodians clean public school buildings, although open school students help. The custodians in the private schools usually are the students and staff. Natural Bridge students took more than a year to figure out a workable system for school cleaning. Jobs were assigned by a daily lottery, and within ten minutes the building would take on a semblance of order. Fifteen minutes later the mess had returned because the students preferred not to go home. It was their school, just as Clonlara and Community belong to their students. Some of the sense of belonging comes with the cleaning. In American traditional schools students have little responsibility for their environment. (On the other hand, their Japanese counterparts sweep the floors and wash the desks and windows of their schools.)

A checklist of resources owned by and/or available to our schools in 1983 is in Chart 5. Small schools have flexibility to fill their needs where they can.

Facts about the size of the schools, their parents and students, their approaches to discipline, and the resources they use are as follows:

1. People make these constructive, interactive learning environments; regardless of their age differences, the students and staff respect and trust one another.
2. The schools are small or organize themselves to feel small and friendly.
3. The schools generate a sense of belonging.
4. Students and parents have chosen these schools.
5. The students are multi-racial and from different backgrounds.
6. Student skills vary.
7. Discipline is not imposed by outside authorities but comes from within.
8. Physical resources are borrowed or invented; people are the most valuable resource.

Chapter 7

FEARS OF PARENTS:
WILL MY CHILD LEARN?

"Will you guarantee my son will get what he needs?" an angry woman asked in an early Natural Bridge planning meeting.

"How do you know your ideas will work?" another insisted.

"The ideas are old and tried. Others have done it," I argued. "I have faith, but you will have to decide for yourself." Parents, students, and teachers take a leap of faith when they cast their lot with a brand new innovative school. Only one fact is clear: the school will be different from those the parents and teachers attended.

After seeing Tetsuko Kuroyanagi's new school in action, a few parents grew frightened and wanted to take their children back to familiar, traditional safety. But the children were excited with learning and did not want to leave. To see beneath the surface veneer of daily school activities the parents had to be able to look beyond their image of what constituted a "school."

These Japanese parents are not very different from a visiting teacher who arrived at Clonlara one morning at 8:30 to diligently observe all the educational proceedings. Three hours later the visitor pulled a teacher aside to ask exactly when school was expected to start.

A new school does not come with guarantees. Although "accountability" and "excellence" are contemporary educational buzzwords, chil-

95

dren in traditional schools are not given guarantees for learning and performance. Traditional education usually blames the child for failing to learn, but seldom faults the school for failing to educate.

Survivors among alternative schools "have gained acceptance as legitimate educational endeavors" (Barr 1981, 555). Traditional schools automatically acquire historical legitimacy by looking and acting like schools of the past. It is not enough that parents and students choose alternative, open schools over traditional education, but the alternative schools must repeatedly prove their legitimacy. Detroit Open School was legitimate from its start because Laurajean Milligan's reputation as an excellent teacher accompanied her into the new program. Innovative programs gain respect through successful evaluation; they constantly are asked to justify their existence, usually by means of test scores.

After many years of performance, our alternative schools have established track records.

To the frustration of well-intentioned researchers, these schools are not easy subjects for study. Philosophically they tend to oppose the research methods most valued by "legitimate" social scientists. Their success at reaching their future-oriented goals can be assessed only after their young students have grown and dispersed—when rounding them up for study is far from simple. A meticulous sixteen-year study was necessary, for example, to prove the cost benefits of preschool education (Berreuta-Clement et al 1984); assessing the effects of our schools on students would take at least as long.

Collecting appropriate information is difficult enough, but organizing the information to reflect the individualized activities and goals of these innovative schools is another challenge. An increase in *average* test scores reveals nothing about Johnny's or Jessica's personal gains, or losses. "We feel that there cannot and should not be summaries of the effects of the open wing on its participants," notes one attempt at evaluating the outcomes of open education (Krasner and Hanley 1984, 207). In lieu of statistics or summaries, this report offers verbatim excerpts from interviews with graduating high school students and their parents from which the reader is to deduce the impact of open elementary education.

The ideal researcher requires the visions in the curriculum crystal ball, patience, inventiveness, and a long life.

This chapter is about students. What happens to them while they attend these schools? What becomes of them in later life?

First we will look at the results of the ubiquitous standardized tests, the form of evaluation least valued by these innovative schools but most respected by traditionalists.

Test Scores

Test makers have developed a plethora of standardized achievement measures. The widely used California Achievement Tests (CAT) consist of multiple choice questions aimed at assessing reading, math, and language skills. Test scores often are reported as "grade equivalents" e.g. grade 1.2 or grade 3.7 or grade 11.9, but grade equivalents are only test scores. A fifth grader whose reading comprehension score is grade equivalent 3.0 cannot be equated with an average beginning third grader. All that can be said is that the fifth grader simply missed many multiple choice questions which his fellow fifth graders answered correctly. Similarly another fifth grader who reads at grade equivalent 11.9 has answered many more questions correctly than her classmates but is not necessarily capable of understanding the same books as a twelfth grader. Test results must be interpreted with caution.

Now, after these caveats, using standardized achievement tests as the measure, do children who go to these innovative schools "learn" as well as students in traditional schools? The answer is yes overall. On the average their test scores are at least as high as their traditionally educated counterparts. Here is some evidence.

A decline in school enrollment in 1979 forced some Ann Arbor elementary schools to combine two grades in one traditional classroom while single-graded classrooms remained the norm and multi-graded informal classrooms continued to flourish. The educational effectiveness of these three types of classroom organization was compared by looking at the gains of third and fifth graders between spring and fall administrations of the CAT. Overall the gains of children in informal classrooms were similar to their traditionally educated age mates. Third graders in informal classrooms excelled in reading comprehension, but fifth graders in traditional multi-age classrooms made the biggest gains in math computation (Ann Arbor Public Schools 1981). The larger gain in reading comprehension is consistent with the informal approach to reading; the larger gain in math computation in the traditional multi-age classrooms remains a puzzle—although possibly the overworked teachers assigned more computational busy work (Ann Arbor Public School, 1981).

In 1983, Ann Arbor open classroom students made greater than expected CAT gains in math between fall and spring. Gains in reading could not be assessed because scores on the first round of tests had been so high that there was no more "up" to go (Ann Arbor Public Schools 1983).

In its early years, Middle Years Alternative was more like the informal, open classrooms than it is today. In the 1977-1978 school year, MYA students scored as well as a matched sample of traditional intermediate school students on the Michigan Educational Assessment Program (MEAP) as well as on the vocabulary, reading comprehension, and math comprehension subtests of the CAT. While the MYA students scored lower in math computation, they reported they liked math more than the students in the regular classes. In fact these MYA students had more positive attitudes towards learning in general than their traditional peers (Thompson and Schein 1978).

Detroit Open School shows an interesting pattern of CAT scores. In this school, student turnover is negligible; once a child manages to get in, he or she stays for years. It is reasonable to expect that the longer a child's experience with open education, the greater the effect. In the early grades, the average scores in reading and mathematics are not very different from the Detroit average, but in grade five the scores of the Open School students begin an upward surge—in 1984 Open School reading average 6.2 vs city average 5.8; math average 6.4 vs 5.9—and never turn back. Open School eighth graders scored 10.4, two grade equivalents higher than the district average. Their math average was 10.0, 1.3 grade equivalents above the district average. These results have to be understood in the context in which the learning took place. Detroit teachers responded to years of declining test scores with a campaign of direct instruction in both test content and skills. The Open School teachers didn't bother with their instructional packets, continued their flowing, non-test oriented curriculum, and still surpassed the traditional programs.

The Detroit Open School shared its building with a traditional elementary neighborhood program for many years before having its own school building. In 1984, the Open School fifth graders scored half a grade equivalent higher on CAT reading and math than their traditional buildingmates whose average score was around the Detroit average.

A review of over one hundred studies revealed no consistent differences between students in open and traditional classrooms on the usual achievement test measures (Horwitz 1979).

Upland Hills Farm School gives no standardized tests, but the Clonlara staff was surprised when ten of their long time students insisted on taking the California Achievement Tests just as their traditionally educated neighbors. These particular students had attended Clonlara at least three grade and test free years, but they still scored well above their expected grade equivalents. Only one student, a girl with neurologically based specific learning difficulties, placed below her grade's average.

Natural Bridge students took the Sequential Tests of Educational Progress (STEP) with what they said was boring regularity. New students suffered through one form in the fall and another in the spring while old Natural Bridgers were tested only once a year. Only on the day of spring testing would a visitor have found everyone quietly and anxiously engaged in the same activity at the same time. Afterwards students were encouraged to compare their answers with the "right" ones. If Kate and Jim thought their scores were unfair, they were encouraged to study the questions and answers and argue about the "correctness" of the test manufacturer's choices. Anyone could repeat a test—although only the first scores were used for statistical analysis—because learning was possible even from standardized achievement tests.

Each year at Natural Bridge, the average increase on most subtests was statistically significant. Spelling scores were an annual embarrassment, however, for they increased little if at all. Scores on math concepts, science, and social studies consistently soared while reading, math computation, study skills, and English expression made more modest gains; all of which was remarkable given the general lack of instruction in these subject matter areas. Math computation actually dropped the year that handheld calculators were strongly encouraged, but the dramatic rise in math concepts more than offset the loss.

HIGH SCHOOL

What about high school students?

When students in a new alternative high school program were compared with matched students in a traditional school on the Iowa Test of Educational Development, no statistically significant differences were found (McCauley and Dornbusch 1978).

Despite Community High's reputation as a haven for oddballs and potential dropouts, approximately 65 percent of its graduates go on to some form of higher education. (That doesn't include the 1980 graduate who simply skipped college, hired a handful of fellow CHS computer freaks, and established his own computer software company.) More than half the students in each of Ann Arbor's three high schools, including Community, take the Scholastic Aptitude Test (SAT). Community students regularly score higher than traditional high school students. In 1982, the Community verbal average was 600, well above the 492 and 488 of the other two high schools, and math was 595, somewhat higher than the 564 and 542 of their local fellows. Community graduates have succeeded in many prestigious colleges and universities including Harvard, Yale, Northwestern, Oberlin, University of Chicago, and the University of Michigan.

ACHIEVEMENT IN COLLEGE

Performance in college is another criterion used to evaluate the effectiveness of earlier education. Unfortunately, the relationship between college grades and later success and self-satisfaction in the real world seems negligible (Jennings and Nathan 1977). Actually, by one report, the best predictor of adult creativity was a student's independent and sustained participation in hobbies and extracurricular activities (Wallach 1972).

The complex relationships between high school curricula and performance in college were detailed in the elegant and convincing Eight-Year Study. Contained in five volumes, this research was published in 1942, unfortunately at a time when World War II had prior claims on our attention, so its findings have not received the attention they deserve.

The Eight-Year Study began in 1930 when the Progressive Education Association met "to consider ways by which the secondary schools of the United States might better serve all our young people" (Aikin 1942, 1). The proposed innovations seemed attractive and feasible but, if carried out, would have threatened students' chances of getting into college. In the 1930s, a college education was for a selected minority—only one out of six students entering high school made the grade. College admission was based on the successful completion of certain high school courses prescribed by the universities; innovation in secondary education would be impossible without changes in college admission policies. (While the study focused on the college educated, the Progressive Education Association hoped secondary education would be as "profoundly significant" to the remaining five.)

In a unique effort, the Progressive Education Association persuaded most of the elite private and prestigious state universities, some two hundred in all, to waive their specific entrance requirements for the graduates of thirty experimental high schools. Twenty-five of these colleges, Harvard, Yale, and the University of Michigan among them, became centers for intensive study.

The thirty experimental high schools committed themselves to creating learning environments in which students worked together at tasks clearly related to their own personal purposes. The thirty geographically diverse schools included public and private, and large and small institutions. Their common concern was dissatisfaction with the work they were doing. "…if attendance at school was to become the stimulating, meaningful experience it could be for each student, they knew that the classroom should become a place of cooperative activity in which teachers and students would seek together to achieve results which they believed important" (Aikin 1942, 18). Students would not amass credits by blindly completing arbitrary course requirements but would "engage in activities which satisfy his desires, work at the solution of problems which he faces in everyday living" (Aikin 17).

With assistance from the project staff, each experimental school independently modified its curricula and learning experiences. The project's evaluation staff further worked closely with teachers and administrators to develop evaluation instruments directly related to the purposes of the high schools, not to college entrance requirements. In the process they produced around two hundred tests of which sixteen were most widely used; these ranged from application of principles, the nature of proof, and record of free reading, to seven modern paintings. Objectives for records and reports were defined and the results became the method of passing information on to colleges.

Much educational research is narrowly conceived or fails to address relevant questions. Investigative efforts may lack control groups or fall short of assessing appropriate student characteristics or achievements. The monumental Eight-Year Study is none of the above. Over four years, 1,475 of its graduates were admitted to universities. Each experimental student was matched painstakingly by sex, age, race, home and community background, interests, and probable future with a control classmate from a traditional high school. These experimental and control students were followed and evaluated throughout their college careers.

In September, 1936, the first graduates of the experimental high schools entered college and later were followed by three more graduating classes. All experimental students and their matchees were observed closely throughout their college careers; they responded to questionnaire after questionnaire and interview after interview. Their teachers and fellow students also were interviewed about their progress. The results were striking.

The students from the thirty experimental schools consistently did better academically than their traditional counterparts. They earned higher grades in all subjects except foreign languages. They received both more academic and more nonacademic honors; they were the club officers, the dramatic leads, the successful athletes.

The experimental students further were judged to be higher in intellectual curiosity and drive, resourcefulness, precision and objectivity in thinking, and awareness of what was happening in the world. The conclusion? "It is quite obvious from these data that the Thirty Schools graduates, as a group, have done a somewhat better job than the comparison group whether success is judged by college standards, by the students' contemporaries, or by the individual students" (Aikin, p. 112).

Some experimental high schools transformed themselves radically while others made only cosmetic alterations. Interestingly, the students from the six most radically changed high schools greatly exceeded their matchees in positive characteristics, and those from the two most radical experimental high schools surpassed their matchees by an even greater margin. Meanwhile the students from the least changed high schools differed little from their matchees.

The conclusion, according to the Dean of Columbia College, was that "the stimulus and the initiative which the less conventional approach to secondary school education affords sends on to college better human material than we have obtained in the past," (Aikin 1942, 150). Professors from Lawrence College, Bryn Mawr, Harvard, Swarthmore, and Chicago signed the report in agreement.

This study was largely overlooked in the educational ferment of the 1970s. Perhaps revolutionaries prefer what is "new" and enjoy reinventing the wheel.

SUCCESS IN LIFE AND OTHER RESEARCH

Margaret Willis was directly involved with the Eight-Year Study as a teacher at the Ohio State University Laboratory School. Twenty years after their graduation she tracked down her old high school students—they had christened themselves guinea pigs. According to their high school test scores the guinea pigs had varied widely in ability, but their teachers—like those in our alternative schools—paid little attention to the differences. Twenty years later they had become an outstanding group of young adults who were atypically active in their communities, often as leaders. They were both creative and autonomous. These mixed ability former Ohio Lab School students were more satisfied with their lives, more likely to be leaders in their professions, and more often mentioned in Who's Who than were Lewis Terman's long studied "geniuses" who were selected on the basis of their high intelligence test scores (Willis 1961).

The other piece of research which convincingly documents the relative effectiveness of different curricular approaches concerns at-risk, disadvantaged preschoolers who were randomly assigned to one of three preschool programs in Ypsilanti, Michigan. When the preschoolers reached the fourth grade, the High/Scope Educational Research Foundation found no differences between children who had been in teacher-directed, open framework, or child-centered preschool programs; all curricular approaches had resulted in improved performances on ability and achievement tests (Weikart et al 1978). But when the former at-risk preschoolers reached their early twenties, differences between the curricular approaches became evident. Those assigned to the two child-initiated programs (open framework and child-centered) were much less likely to have been involved in delinquent acts than those in the teacher-directed program. They also were more likely to have participated more in sports and extracurricular activities (Salmans 1989). The child-initiated preschool programs may have facilitated a sense of personal responsibility while the children in the teacher-directed program were given no responsibility.

One of the booby traps awaiting any researcher eager to compare the outcomes of open and traditional education is definitional. The High/Scope research was carefully designed and controlled, but others play fast and loose with important variables. All schools labelled "open" are not the same. For some, open education is that which goes on in a building without interior walls. Others claim that walls make no difference and that open refers to relationships between students and teachers. With so much diversity in what researchers have variously defined as open education, perhaps it is surprising that a review of more than one hundred studies comparing children in open and traditional education yielded any consistent results. In most of the studies the different outcomes from type of schooling either were statistically insignificant or decidedly mixed. Any differences tended to favor the open school students who were found to have more favorable attitudes toward school and to be more creative, curious, cooperative and independent than their traditionally educated peers (Horwitz 1979). These results are consistent with the findings of the Eight-Year Study.

Informally our schools are aware of their achievements. Each and every child may not flourish, but most do. That's what former Upland

Hills students report to their old teachers. Clonlara often hears from long gone but not forgotten students and parents about the significance of their Clonlara experience. So does Detroit Open School. Students from every graduating class came back to attend Community High School's tenth reunion and many more shared their feelings in letters.

Most Natural Bridge students returned to traditional schools after their middle school sojourn. "How will they ever be able to go back to regular schools?" was a nagging question, and by its second year we began to find out how its former students withstood the shock of reentry. "School is fine," Sarah wrote from her new school in a new community. "I had no trouble adjusting. But sometimes I feel like telling a teacher to shut up. I'm doing well and am ahead of most of the kids. I'm ahead in French, math, and English. My teachers are all nice except English and he is really dumb; I mean he's smart, but he's really mental." If grades are a criterion, after one, two, three or even four years of not being graded, the students did at least as well after "going back" as they did before their Natural Bridge experience. Many did much better. It seemed as if most had learned that they controlled their own learning and that their choices and decisions had consequences. Back in traditional school they might not like a homework assignment but they would choose to complete it because the option was worth neither their time nor energy. In order to free the time and energy to assume more important challenges it sometimes is easier to do a meaningless task than to fight. These students had begun to think about their own personal goals.

In spite of her low math test scores, Amy's shift from Upland Hills to a traditional public school was fairly easy. There she not only learned the math she needed, but also won science and math awards before entering the University of Michigan in pre-medicine—where her problems began. In this alien environment "the curve" determined grades in huge lecture classes, and only a select few were rewarded with grades worthy of graduate school. Appalled by the competitive atmosphere, Amy transferred to a small college. Upland Hills graduates tend to opt for smaller colleges like Sarah Lawrence with a thousand students, or Hampshire College with twelve hundred, instead of the University of Michigan with its twenty-four thousand undergraduates and ten thousand graduate students. Although the admission requirements to these three schools are similar, the feeling of daily life must be very different.

Nevertheless, the ingenious products of alternative education may even be able to find personalized, meaningful education at places like the University of Michigan. While pre-med and some other areas of major concentration may be impossible, one Community High graduate took advanced math courses with only a handful of students and another seldom had a class with an enrollment over twenty-five because he talked his way into low enrollment advanced courses. Another Community graduate found "Introduction to Ancient Greek" the perfect course for her with only four students, and the opportunity to handle original ancient materials—the lure of experiential learning does not diminish with age.

Students from alternative schools do succeed when they return to traditional education. According to the Eight-Year Study and the follow-ups on Ohio Lab School graduates and Ypsilanti preschoolers, they tend to do better both in school and in life-at-large than traditionally educated youth.

ELITISM

"This school isn't for everyone," Laurajean Milligan says over lunch. "We've never insisted a student leave, but if the parents have no faith in what we're doing, then the student disappears. It doesn't happen often because we work hard at helping everyone understand our approach to education."

None of our private schools refuses to admit one type of student or another. Applicants are not tested to see if they will make the school grade—whatever that may be. The public programs are open to all comers and the students are admitted either first-come/first-serve, or by lottery. Depending on available space, these schools accept all who are interested—although the private schools may have financial limitations. And yet they are accused of being subject to creeping elitism.

Who should attend these schools? Could they be "bad" for some children and "good" for others?

Our alternative schools would agree they work best for those families and students who understand and believe their philosophy and goals. A few students who came to Natural Bridge from the many freedoms of an underground, private elementary school were a delight; they were eager to learn about everything, except math, but with teacher patience and cajoling they even took that on. But what of the others? Before enrolling in Natural Bridge School, students were encouraged to visit for a day. They seldom wanted to leave, but their parents had more difficulty making the leap of faith.

And yet prospective parents and students might be counseled to more appropriate learning arrangements elsewhere. Although he was a junior in high school, Mark's specific learning disability had kept his reading at a CAT grade equivalent of 2.1. The test score and low reading level were not problems in themselves, however; a student with similar reading and writing deficits already was learning and gaining confidence at Natural Bridge. The problem was that Mark's only satisfactions in school came from those very things which Natural Bridge lacked: a competitive intermural athletic program, a large brass band, and other sixteen-year-olds. Even with unceasing teacher attention he would have been lonely, dissatisfied, and still unable to read well. He and his family were referred to tutors and other possible schools.

"I wonder," a critic muses, "if all these supposedly successful students would have done just as well in educational snakepits. They probably would have succeeded whatever happened to them." Many would have survived immersion in snakes or tigers, perhaps, but their energy would have been sapped in the effort. Others would have perished, convinced they were doomed failures. The evidence, both informally and from research, indicates open education touches student lives in many ways.

At Upland Hills nine-year-old Kenneth turned teacher and gave the visitor a nonstop demonstration lecture on automobile construction. Car manuals and auto parts poured out of his knapsack. When his adult pupil failed to understand a point, he led her to the old car he and other students were dismantling. In his former school this bubbling, excited boy had been a daydreamer who seldom finished assignments. Before attending Clonlara, Rod had survived five years of traditional education with good reports and growing reluctance to attend school. Valued for being himself instead of for the grades he received, Rod exploded into learning and exploration at Clonlara.

Perhaps neither Kenneth nor Rod would have perished in traditional schools, but Jenny had chosen a narrow, destructive path. At fourteen she vowed to marry an out-of-work high school dropout as soon as legally possible, and the only use for school was to research the state with the lowest legal age for marriage. After two Natural Bridge years not only had she forgotten about running off to Georgia, but she succeeded well enough in a traditional high school to graduate a year early. When last heard from she was studying pharmacy in college. A 1975 Community High graduate, now a professional musician, wrote his alma mater on its tenth anniversary. "I nearly dropped out in the ninth grade," he reported.

"The next year I went to CHS. The atmosphere at CHS let me reopen myself to learning. I left feeling that if I wished to accomplish something, I would be able to seek out any additional knowledge and use it to reach my goal—a feeling of confidence."

The parent of a second grader listed the changes open education had brought to her son: "1. No more headaches! 2. He is more relaxed. He likes school. He's no longer obsessed with who is good or bad. He isn't afraid he won't finish his work—before he even starts. He trusts the kids more—'Mom, they don't go crazy when the teacher is out of the room.'" A sixth grader's parent reported, "The OCP teachers have avoided recording negative labels for him even when he sometimes caused problems so other teachers won't have a pre-set notion that he'll cause problems. Over time the OCP teachers have moved his behavior from problematic to, for the most part, that of an eager and responsible student by helping him channel his energies."

Parents sometimes use their children to fight their own battles. Three children from one family attended Clonlara a few months before leaving in anger. Clonlara had tried to deal with these disruptive people, but the mother insisted the school had failed them. Later Pat Montgomery learned Clonlara was the fourth school in two years to be rejected by the family. In time the children might have succeeded but the parent would not let it happen.

Many dream that these schools are for everyone. The reality is somewhat different The failure usually is not with the child or the student; high school students, however, must bear a greater responsibility for their own behaviors than their juniors.

Reconciliation may be impossible when the values and expectations of the parents and the realities of the school have no common meeting ground. When one of these schools excludes a student, the reasons are complex and specific to the particular situation. At age ten John had a long history of disrupting his class in general and talking back to teachers in particular. At Clonlara his math skills proved good and he was a fair reader, but he specialized in taking on the very worst qualities of his fellow students. He was easily provoked into hitting others, and his hostility towards females fueled long school meetings. He told large and small lies to protect himself, but none of this was reason enough for him to leave the school. His single mother had to work long hours to try to make a success of her business, and John's busy childhood hadn't included much time for play. John simply hadn't learned how to live with others. In

Clonlara's free atmosphere he worked on that which he needed most. He played. He socialized. And his mother worried that he would "fall behind" in school work and insisted on homework. Because school assignments never were enough she bought workbooks and assigned hours of work each night. The school and the parent were locked in conflict. John wanted to stay, but his mother and the Clonlara staff agreed it would be best if he went to another school.

These idealistic schools feel anguish when they fail to meet the needs of each and every student.

Another reality is that schools of choice attract students and parents with many agendas and many problems.

SELFISH STUDENTS

Won't these children who follow their own interests and take their education smoothly and sweetly in individually tailored packets turn into selfish, self-centered creatures? Won't they expect the world to revolve around them? These pervasive fears haunt parents who have observed the cold, cruel nature of the world and believe calluses are the only protection for their children.

An environment where each person freely follows individual desires without regard for others is horrible to contemplate. Yet imagining a group of children acting in such a manner is almost impossible. Humans of all ages are social creatures.

A fundamental goal of open alternative education is that students learn to live socially and responsibly with knowledge of and concern for others. At Upland Hills children learn about their interdependence with nature and their connections to people everywhere. Participation in problem solving discussions is Clonlara's sole requirement. Natural Bridge students worked to solve their unending school social problems and contributed their volunteer work to the community.

An eight-year-old sweeps up spilled sand in the Detroit Open School kindergarten. "I'm not in kindergarten, you know," she explains shyly, "I like it here." She had asked her teacher if she could help the younger children, and throughout the school, children of all ages are helping children of all ages.

These children, like those in the Eight-Year Study, excel in social concern and participation. Freed from the competition found in traditional schools, students are able to learn in cooperation.

Shared learning at Upland Hills Farm School. Photograph by Alex Korn.

Summary

The achievement test scores of students who have experienced open alternative education tend to be at least as high as those of their traditional counterparts. Many attend college. Evidence exists for their becoming individuals with greater than average enthusiasm for learning, intellectual curiosity and drive, resourcefulness, precision and objectivity in thinking, awareness of world happenings, creativity, cooperation, and independence.

With a few significant exceptions, consistent *proof* that students developed these wonderful qualities because they attended these schools is lacking, but so also is the counterproof.

Students adapt to traditional education after attending these schools with little or no difficulty. Many seem to be strengthened by their sojourn off the beaten path.

Students who have severe problems adjusting to these schools tend to be caught in an abyss between parental expectations of what schools should be and what the real school is. When a school's daily deviations from its idealistic philosophy become apparent to a purist advocate of free and open education, his child might be forced to leave the compromised program. More often, traditionally educated parents may want to transfer their children to more familiar learning environments after they have witnessed the exciting ambiguities of open education in action.

Students in these alternative schools commonly develop a strong sense of self-worth, but their self-esteem is used neither to elevate themselves nor to demean others. By appreciating their own value, they are better able to value and feel concern for others.

Chapter 8

MORE WORRIES

Looking at fears about open-ended education is a little like opening Pandora's Box. Worries beget more worries.

The last chapter discussed the long term outcomes of traveling alternative educational paths. In the long run children not only survive but often flourish. But what happens to students and teachers en route? What do they do all day? Young children treat these schools as a natural extension of their lives, but the expectations of their elders already have been set in a matrix of experience. Fear is a companion of those stepping into the unknown.

FREEDOM AND THE STUDENT

"Is this true? Are there actually schools like this?" asked a Japanese university graduate who had just translated Yasushi Ohnuma's descriptions of Denmark's Friskollen 70 and Michigan's Clonlara School. "If I had been given so much freedom, I never would have gone to classes. How can it be that these children learn what they need?" We have seen that students do learn, but how do they deal with the daily freedom and responsibilities?

When a third grade boy first comes to Clonlara he grabs eagerly at freedom. The power to decide his own activities has been placed firmly in his hands, and usually he chooses to stay away from anything he decides is "work." If, by chance, he loves to read, he might indulge in a reading orgy. More often children new to the school run and play indoors and out. Older youth run and play, too, but their chief activity is incessant socializing, talking, whispering, sharing secrets.

There are other reactions, too. In her first weeks at Clonlara, Susan complained bitterly that Pat Montgomery didn't like her because she never told her what to do. So Pat accommodated her and said, "Open your textbook to page nineteen and get to work." Little by little Susan would learn to tolerate more freedom.

Initially the Natural Bridge students were so grateful to be free from the restrictions of their former schools that their teachers could do no wrong. The students themselves were cooperative, productive, and unfailingly cheerful, but all that changed. While they continued to come to school early and leave late, they also took to complaints, arguments, and tears. Everything was boring; no one followed through with decisions or plans, least of all their own. The staff was afraid they had failed before they had begun and were angry at the miserable, angry students. Only when this confrontation with freedom and decisions had been identified and was open to discussion could the staff and students begin to work together. Both could begin to identify the obstacles in their chosen route.

A student whose every school minute has been scheduled and controlled may feel lost and out of control without the familiar, hated restrictions. A partial solution includes a public, cooperative search for and labelling of both freedoms and responsibilities.

Each of the schools we have seen has achieved its own balance point between absolute freedom and authoritarian control. At Upland Hills each morning, the students are expected to work on their interrelated basic skills, after which they can make decisions and choices from the daily offerings of activities. At Clonlara group meetings are required of all, and older students are expected to attend classes.

Detroit Open School helps students adjust to its freedoms by increasing them throughout the school year. The school corridors and rooms are different in September than in May. In the spring the elementary students flow back and forth through open doors and fill the corridors and any other space, as they select many of their own activities and certainly determine their own schedules. In the fall most students remain within their classrooms, doors closed, setting their own schedule to complete a certain number of teacher designed tasks. This slow, controlled loosening of freedom may be necessary for everyone's survival in this large school with big classes. In a small school, however, it may be possible to loosen the limits for everyone right away, then fine tune to meet individual needs and responses. Change is not immediate. With patience, time, and understanding, students gradually begin to feel the stirring of unfamiliar needs. They want to expand their horizons. They begin to think for themselves and ask questions. They let themselves be involved in the school's activities.

When Randy first came to Natural Bridge, he specialized in running, friendly wrestling, and, sometimes, when everyone else was busy and involved, sitting in a corner waiting to entrap a companion in goofing off. There were classes and activities he might have enjoyed if he had allowed himself, but he had committed himself to doing nothing "constructive" or "educational." Randy's problem was that doing nothing was boring. Because he was too lazy to move, he sat in his corner through an American History class, then a math class in which he alone understood a principle of decimals. Finally, he became a regular participant in math, and next week he joined dissection and Randy was hooked on learning.

A teacher often must be a mindreader, able to sense when a Randy or a Susan is ready to try something new, to become involved, to begin to learn how to become a self-directed learner. Mindreading is a high level skill seldom mentioned in schools of education. Yet this intuitive awareness may be as natural as breathing to the best teachers of any nation.

Clonlara's portable classroom was crammed with excited people on the last day of a week long visit by ten Japanese teachers. It was a time for giving gifts, singing, and playing noisy games, and scarcely anyone noticed five-year-old Edward slip in the door with a huge lunchbox and a very worried look. What has happened to my world, he seemed to be saying, as he wandered into the room and lay face down on the floor. A Japanese teacher did notice, and soon Edward was watching the games from the safety of Mr. Watanabe's lap. The teacher gently clasped the boy's hands, and together they clapped in rhythm, softly, then more vigorously, until Edward was able to participate, at first with his friend's support, and then alone. With few words in common, the teacher had sensitively helped the boy become part of the group, to learn from others, and, finally, to participate.

To summarize:

1. Each student reacts to sudden freedom from restrictions and regula-

tions in her or his own manner. Many act as if a heavy lid had been lifted from a boiling pot; they splash in all directions as they test the reality of promises

2. The students are subject to strange feelings and unexpected reactions as they learn to live effectively with their new freedoms.
3. The youngest children, the preschoolers, the kindergartners, even first graders, usually adapt most easily.
4. Students may be helped to make the transition from unquestioning conformist to self-motivated seeker by the company of other students already accustomed to freedom, by flexible and sensitive teachers, through scheduling adjustments, and by a gradual expansion of freedoms and choice.

Freedom and the Teacher

Children may be able to adjust, but what happens to a teacher accustomed to a traditional role, one who is comfortable with a set curriculum and excels in firm control of his or her class? What feelings wrack a teacher who values wise use of time when three students are in a tree, two more are eating their lunches at ten in the morning, and a few more are reading comic books under a table? What happens to a teacher accustomed to providing teacher directed learning activities every school second?

First, teachers must be committed to the goals of their schools. Like their students they must want to be there. If they believe students and teachers should have friendly, two-way relationships, they will begin to move towards that goal.

In reality teachers may fear loss of status and loss of control. However, relinquishing power does not lead automatically to the loss of respect; the student respects the respectful teacher for the person within the teacher. Children are able to see behind professional masks, to identify the bullying and ignorant or the weak and approval seeking, to value the understanding, informed, and honest. When teachers are able to be open, to tell the students in actions and words of their respect and trust, control becomes a false issue.

"What will we do today?" is a pressing daily question for teachers and students alike. If there is no prescribed curriculum, what will happen at 8 A.M., at 11 A.M., at 2 P.M.? What happens depends on the people there. What happens one day is related to what happened the day before, and, although the first day is the most difficult, there is a little first day in each subsequent day. The preparations for each new day depend in part on the ages and developmental levels of the students, and on the skills, interests, and abilities of the staff, all of which may not reassure a nervous teacher or parent.

The teacher of younger children gives a great deal of thought and time to arranging the environment which the child explores at his or her own rate. The teacher is present as a helper and a stimulus to the child's exploration; he or she is a sensitive radar receiver ever alert to the needs of the students and interferes only when needed. "When needed" probably differs for each teacher and even for each child. Six-year-old John, for example, has no self-confidence and constantly begs for adult help. So each day his teacher waits a little longer to give special attention to the assurance seeking John, then praises him for being himself, a boy who can try so many things. Perhaps he has fit most of the pieces in a puzzle, or built a wobbly block tower, or written his name or thought of a word he wanted to learn to read. Gradually he finds he can do more for himself. Most young children have such a great desire to learn that they do not have to be force fed. They want to solve their own educational mysteries.

The teacher of older children, roughly age ten and up, has more complex problems. Critics of open-ended education have voiced the suspicion that these teachers are lazy and that all they do is arrive at school daily and declare, "Here I am. Let me know if you want to learn anything." Actually the teacher has been planning and arranging long before the school day starts. If the school environment is filled with a variety of books and materials and other possibilities, including other students, both teacher and students may be satisfied, at least for a while. But without sensitive adult participation in their school lives most older students will become bored and restless. They need the understanding and knowledge of their teachers. They need the stimulation, excitement, and ideas of their elders. Their teachers should bring commitment to the school's goals, understanding of the skills and needs of their students, and plans for potential activities compatible to both.

Fortunately this teacher is seldom alone. The staffs in these schools work as teams to help one another create exciting learning environments. Planning together is one of the most important uses of adult time and energy.

"Well," says the teacher still looking for answers. "All that's fine, but just what will I be doing on Monday when I walk into that classroom?"

Let's go back a step. Long before a teacher enters this new school world, he or she will have been reading—possibly John Holt's book *What Will I Do on Monday?* (1970)—and thinking and sharing ideas with others. Ideally the teacher will have seen and experienced daily life in similar schools. The teacher brings her or his own skills, interests, and passions to the classroom for, like the students, a teacher is not a blank slate. On the first Monday the teacher will bring a collection of developmentally appropriate tentative plans. The teacher first will try that which is most comfortable and see what happens. Perhaps the teacher thinks journal writing might be a good place to start. Perhaps the teacher would like to build a school garden or a school bank or a school business. If a teacher's wonderful plan falls flat on its face for lack of interest, she or he will swallow hard and ask for help and advice from the students who may have their own awakening ideas. The teacher's own skills and knowledge are a springboard to future planning. Because they always are stepping into the unknown, these teachers always feel that edge of excitement that comes from uncertainty, but no one can function effectively in profound fear. The teacher begins in the real present and moves ahead a step at a time.

It is an exciting process. A new teacher, experienced in traditional education, observed, "You know, it's strange. If you teach where everything is decided for you, you spend all your time fighting against the restrictions. And if you and the students have freedom to decide, you spend all your time and energy trying to get something going."

Even the most dedicated open education advocates will find themselves reacting at times just as their own teachers had. Although they are committed to allowing students to live and learn at their own rates, their stomachs will twist and they will be angered by unappreciative students who are "wasting time." What is Randy learning while he sits in a corner, idly turning the pages of a comic book? How can those girls talk and whisper for *three solid hours*? And what about Kevin who seems to be sleeping? Teachers should know they will revert to their old ways from time to time. They often worry. Automatically they will order a Randy to get to work right this minute, or else. The clever student will respond, "Or else what?" and then it is time for everyone to get together and reexamine their purposes.

Beginning teachers can expect to be inconsistent. For a time the Natural Bridge staff would be completely accepting of anything the students did, or did not, choose to do. "You can decide," was this laissez faire message, followed shortly by the authoritarian opposite, "You will do what I say, and no arguments." It took time and constant effort to balance between these extremes.

Struggling MYA teachers once returned to traditional methods and had several "troublemaking" students expelled. Long before their final rejection, these students had sensed the disapproval of both teachers and their peers and had nicknamed themselves the Rogues. Rogues were expected to be wild and break rules, so they had nothing to lose by living up to their reputations. A school which is functioning well would not have allowed this to continue. If some students feel inferior and isolated, the learning of all is threatened; it is a problem to be tackled positively by everyone.

The teachers themselves must be self-motivated. They do not get the instant glow and reward from finishing a textbook or tying up a unit of study. There is no predictable time in a day, a semester, or a school year when he or she can sit back and feel a sense of completion. Education in these future oriented schools is a process, always incomplete, always moving. Teacher satisfaction comes in unscheduled bursts when he or she notices that today one or even five students are researching their own problems when two months ago they neither could formulate questions nor move independently to seek answers.

In helping their students learn to accept responsibility for themselves, these teachers assume much more personal responsibility than their traditional colleagues. Often they must stand back to observe the changes in their students over time, to see their growth in confidence, critical and analytical thinking, curiosity, flexibility, self awareness, maturity, and the list goes on.

If it is any consolation, the teacher has many potential companions who already have traveled far along this school route. Because each person, every community, differs, the journey is never the same twice. Guides are able to point out major landmarks but not to anticipate each twist and turn. Fifty years ago, the thirty schools of the Eight-Year Study struggled with their confusions. "At the beginning of the Eight-Year Study all of us were rather frantic in our new undertaking. We wanted to do everything, omit nothing. That, of course, was wrong," reported a teacher who went on to say that everyone learned so much from experience that the beginning efforts seemed laughable (Aikin 1942, 27).

All involved with these schools experience successes, make mistakes, and learn from both. A five-year veteran Clonlara preschool teacher observed that the greatest gain he had made there was his own personal growth. "That wouldn't have happened in other schools," he declared. Points in this section include:

1. Teachers new to open education may have to make more adjustments than their students.
2. Teachers must be committed to their school's goals and philosophy.
3. Teachers need not fear loss of control when students and teachers respect one another and grow in mutual trust.
4. No definitive teacher's manual provides directions for daily activities. The teacher brings his or her own skills, knowledge, experience to the process of each day and uses them as a springboard to future planning *with the students.*
5. Not only do teachers have colleagues with whom to share thoughts and plan, but also companions through history.
6. Teachers should expect to find themselves acting at times exactly like the traditional teachers they are trying not to be. Despite their best intentions, they will be inconsistent.
7. The work is demanding and hard, but the possibilities for growth and development are unlimited.

MARCHING TO THE BEAT OF A DIFFERENT DRUMMER

"I like MYA," said eighth grader Mike, "but we've got a problem."
"What is it?"
"It's the others, the regular students. They think we're weird. Because we don't have all the tests and junk they have, they call us babies."

Being different, being part of a minority, too often means being misunderstood. The problems are not insurmountable, but they exist. One student suggested that the MYA students and the traditional students with whom they share both building and classes should establish diplomatic relations, just like two neighboring countries.

The Region Four Open School students so overwhelmed the traditional students with whom they shared a building in learning, enthusiasm, and sheer numbers that there was no real conflict between them. A few years earlier, however, an actual line painted on the floor—the open school teachers christened it the Maginot Line—separated the two programs. The war zone started beyond that yellow stripe on the gray corridor. Once battles raged, but even before the open school gained control of the building, the skirmishes had become only minor events such as this: In the hallway, five open school seventh and eighth graders are practicing a play they have written when a traditional teacher dashes out of the principal's office. "You are not supposed to be here," she commands.

"Our teacher said we could," a boy answers mildly.

"You go back to your room and don't talk back," the teacher orders, then turns on heel and hurries to the traditional wing. Smiling just a little, the students watch her go and return to their rehearsal.

A newspaper article about Upland Hills Farm School once was displayed on the bulletin board in the teachers' room shared by the few MYA teachers and their many traditional colleagues. Within days the clipping was covered with abusive comments. "Stories like this make me feel sick," one said. "Their hardest class must be toilet training," said another.

Separate facilities are a real advantage to schools such as these. Unfortunately too many people are threatened by something different. It almost seems as if they are both angry and jealous when students actually enjoy school. Perhaps they feel it is wrong or even sinful that children are able to learn without the suffering they experienced.

The children, parents, and teachers who march to the beat of this different drummer must put up with some static. They hear what others whisper about them but stick to their chosen path.

At Clonlara the students who asked to take the California Achievement Tests may have been looking for reassurance. Phil Moore's Upland Hills Farm students were worried both about taking final examinations and about returning to traditional schools. The truth is that these students may be concerned about going to "different" schools, but, day by day they feel they own their schools and that there could be none better. Sometimes they set out to test themselves. Ellen had gone to Clonlara all her school days when she decided she would like to try a traditional public school for the sixth grade, just to see what it was like. Successful and satisfied, she returned to Clonlara at the end of the year.

Time may bring perspective to school experience. A 1976 graduate of Community High School, now an accountant, wrote in 1982, "This sounds trite, but I would say that Community High School was a turning point in my life. I could write a novel on how it helped all aspects of my life, but the most important was my self-respect."

Those who march to the beat of a different drummer by participating in these schools do, themselves, feel different.

1. Traditional teachers and students may be both envious and fearful of

these nontraditional students and teachers.
2. Students and teachers in open programs which share buildings with traditional programs may experience disapproval and even warfare.
3. While students sometimes feel sensitive about being "different," from day to day they feel they are fortunate to go to "their" schools.

EXPENSE

The purportedly great expense of alternative open education often is cited as a supposedly rational reason for not developing and supporting such programs. Yet on the whole, these schools do not cost more than their traditional counterparts. The private open schools cost much less to run per pupil than do public traditional schools in the same communities.

In 62 percent of twelve hundred surveyed public alternative secondary schools, the per pupil costs are the same or less than those of the other local traditional programs. This is true, despite the fact that they are small schools, 69 percent enrolling fewer than two hundred students (Raywid 1983). The student/teacher ratio tends to be low in all these public schools, so any lower costs must come from reduced expenses for buildings and equipment. This pattern fits the schools we have visited.

Public education would not support school programs significantly more expensive than the traditional ones. Our schools are under constant pressure to prove themselves both cheaper and better than their more popular counterparts. We have seen that they may receive monies or support services they don't need or want—a specialist teacher at the Region Four Open School or a hot lunch program at Community High School—while they must pinch and scrape to finance the field trips and small classes they need.

The only increased expense in the first year of the Ann Arbor Open Classroom Program was for transportation. Students from the entire city were eligible to attend and bus transportation had to be provided for them. A scheduling adjustment which allowed the buildings that housed the Open Classroom Program to begin and end the school day earlier lessened the costs.

If Community High School or any of the private schools insisted on a physical plant and resources exactly the same as those of the traditional schools, large playing fields, fully equipped auditoriums, swimming pools and gymnasiums, access to expensive individual musical instruments and practice halls, in addition to their small size and low student/teacher ratio, they would be very expensive to operate. But we have seen that these schools almost pride themselves on finding the resources they need without paying for them. An excellent model is provided by the two teachers who staff the Community Resource Office and provide hundreds of diverse courses for the students.

Students, parents, and staff work together to maintain and improve their schools. On a spring night, two dozen young people with their parents and teachers could have been found painting Community High's dingy corridor walls. Some of the young people even had graduated a few years earlier. One October, the father of two boys who had left Clonlara for a traditional junior high school could be found mending a leaky Clonlara roof. He said, "My boys got more from this school than could ever be repaid by tuition money or work," he said, "so I'm here just to express appreciation."

Understanding the precise education costs for each pupil in a public school system, or, even worse, in a given public school, is difficult to say the least. There are too many different budget lines and methods of depreciation and accounting. But for a point of comparison, the *Ann Arbor News* reported on April 4, 1983 that the per pupil expenditure in Ann Arbor was $3,300 per year and in Detroit $2,634 per year. Another report in the October 27, 1983 *Ann Arbor News* states that the Ann Arbor school district actually spent $4,191 per student in the 1982-1983 fiscal year. This larger number probably is more accurate. By contrast, Upland Hills Farm School managed to be self-supporting on the $2,200 tuition per year for each student. This is similar to the per pupil expenses at Natural Bridge School, although tuition charged never equalled the expense. Clonlara's budget is complicated by the extensive home based education program. In 1977 the annual expense per pupil was $864. In 1986 the parent/student/staff board decided to raise the annual tuition to $2,000. Twenty-five percent of the students do not pay full tuition.

Contrary to rumor, open school programs usually cost no more than traditional schools; often they cost much less. To exist they must trim all visible and invisible surplus from their spending. They are masters at stretching dollars.

This chapter has addressed student and teacher reactions to confrontations with freedom and responsibility; it has surveyed their feelings about participating "different" schools and laid to rest the myth that open education must be more costly than traditional schools.

Chapter 9

SURVIVAL NEEDS

Lightning bolts stabbed the night sky and thunderous explosions shook the house in which eighteen people had gathered with newsprint and felt-tip markers at the ready. The dean of Community High School, frustrated informal classroom teachers, professors from the University of Michigan School of Education, parents of young children, and veterans of Parents for Alternative Learning Situations (PALS) had come together to write a proposal to place before the Ann Arbor school board for the creation of what would become first the Open Classroom Program and later Bach Open School. On that stormy night these veterans of the fight for open education struggled with the question of what the program required to succeed. Eleven needs were identified.

*1. Program coordinator or administrator.
*2. Staffing by outside hiring or transfer only with teachers committed to the informal education philosophy.
*3. Supportive in-service programs for the teachers in:
    a. Group process
    b. Communication skills
    c. Use of community resources and volunteers
    d. Informal teaching techniques
4. Flexibility to use diverse methods and materials chosen by teachers and students to work towards their goals.

   *5. Control of some percentage of the classroom budget.
    6. Community resources used both within the school and out in the community.
    7. Teachers committed to successful learning experiences for all children in the program.
   *8. Accessibility of program to all who choose it.
   *9. Active recruitment of students heterogeneous in race, culture, socio-economic status, ability, and age.
  *10. A physical environment conducive to communication, integration of subjects, and experiential learning.
   11. Acknowledgement by the school board that parents and students in the Ann Arbor public school system should have choice in the form and style of education.

This list reflects the frustrations of the lonely informal classroom teachers who sometimes felt like pariahs in their own schools. In those days, in-service training was geared chiefly to making teacherproof curricula fail-safe. Whenever informal classroom students became too enthusiastic and boisterous, the traditional teachers and principals with whom they shared the building complained. At the time of the meeting, only five teachers were persisting in identifying themselves as teaching in informal classrooms.

Over the next two years, the school board was prodded and politicked into approving a policy which made educational alternatives both recognized and legal—thus making the eleventh need a reality. The parents and teachers followed the directives of the board policy, submitted a detailed proposal for an Open Classroom Program, and were informed that they were not qualified to initiate such educational proposals. The school board asked the central administration to develop the program and the original plan was weakened by survival compromises.

Eventually a modified Open Classroom Program did open, but the requirements marked above with an *asterisk either did not come to pass, or were so diluted as to have been made meaningless.

Nontraditional public programs are not easy to start and they may be even harder to maintain. Many forces work to weaken them, to make them more traditional, more familiar. Yet the estimated number of alternative public schools in the United States increased from a mere hundred or so in 1970 to more than ten thousand in 1980. Approximately three million students then were enrolled in alternative public programs (Raywid, 1981). All are not like the schools we have visited, but many share common goals.

Five basic factors have been identified as contributing longevity of decade-old alternative programs: 1) they are attractive to students and parents, 2) they have a clear goal focus, 3) important educators recognize their legitimacy, 4) their funding is reliable, 5) they have created positive school climates (Case, 1981). A positive school climate is an ephemeral mixture of mutual trust and respect, a curriculum which fits the students and allows for success, staff commitment, and access to decision making.

The relative impact of these five factors differs in public and private programs, but all our schools face similar problems. One of the most difficult is decision making.

GOVERNANCE

In traditional education the authoritarian line of decision making is clear and uncluttered. In our schools, and others like them, lines of authority are like tangled webs lying in wait to entrap students, teachers, parents, and administrators.

A school may reach a philosophical consensus that everyone will share in all decisions, but still be unable to agree on a process. Many of the schools enthusiastically founded in the sixties and early seventies were confident that everyone could sit down together and solve any problem—at least they were confident at first. Soon enough they discovered that even good people disagree, about almost anything, and that very few good, bad, or intermediate people thrive on endless, frustrating meetings.

One honest accounting reported that their "all school" meetings (by the third month only four people showed up) "bogged down in numerous minor decisions, petty arguments, hard feelings, shyness, and a general sense that nothing significant ever happened" (Murphy 1978, 144).

Excerpted from a log of a troubled parent-originated school, this lurid example of a five-hour meeting may be edifying. "Despite the great number of outstanding problems, the meeting never gets beyond mutual soul baring, philosophizing, complaining about the 'air of crisis' and debating the relative merits of Pampers versus diapers and organic versus 'junk' food for lunch. After considerable deliberation, consensus is declared (it is not achieved)" on diapers and health food. Both decisions were reversed within a month (Duke 1978, 180).

Without defined procedures for participation, decisions made in any meeting may be overturned in that same meeting after the arrival of an opinionated latecomer. Even worse, nonattending dissidents may try to boobytrap completed decisions they disfavor either indirectly (guerilla warfare) or directly (reversing them in subsequent meetings).

Positive school climate is built on effective and satisfying shared decision making, but not all decisions can be made by a group. In fact, few people, particularly satisfied parents or busy adolescents, enjoy constant participation in administrative trivia. All-school town meetings were to be the driving decision making force at Community High, but after initial success, attendance dropped so sharply that the town meetings lost their value. Decisions had to be made. The dean was responsible for the school and so the dean made decisions. Then the parents who deeply believed in the founding premises of total participation objected. Although different forms of representative government have evolved over the years, this area remains one of potential tension. Each year there is a different mix of students, parents, and staff requiring new approaches to old problems.

A very small unit with no more than twenty-five to thirty students and two or three teachers can work together effectively. But when there are more students and their many parents and their more numerous teachers, the process of governance may be smoothed by establishing well-defined committees. Setting committee agendas requires time and should include representation from all different constituencies.

The breadth of participation depends on the nature of the task, the developmental levels of the students, the time line for decisions, and even the personalities of those involved. Crises do not wait for committees to convene. Administrators may have to act first and get approval later. If they are not trusted and their decisions are displeasing, they will find themselves in the middle of a war.

Making decisions is not enough. "One important tenet of democratic administration is that action should follow full deliberation" (Aikin 1942, 36). If nothing is done after actions are decided upon, the process is empty. The staff in a failing school, for example, decided that a troublesome teacher should be fired or let go. Several months later that teacher was still attending the interminable final meetings. "No one on the staff had told him of the decision that he had to go, no one had felt such a task was his responsibility, and no mechanism existed for dealing intelligently with such problems" (Graubard 1972, 170).

The parents in the Open Classroom Program often faced this deadlock. Although they, sometimes joined by teachers, were allowed to make decisions, they had neither the power nor procedures to carry them out. They possessed neither an administrator of their own nor access to effective substitutes.

The boundaries of parental authority often were tested under fire. Parental energy had created the Open Classroom Program. Parental energy raised the money needed for field trips. Some parents felt that they should be able to mandate the types and destinations of field trips for all children. The teachers were grateful for the energy (and money), but resented the potential interference. Resolution of this issue required hour after hour of meetings at which many close and contradictory votes flipflopped under pressure, and throughout which group awareness slowly developed concerning the participants' complex feelings and competing desires. Consensual agreement was an unattainable ideal.

All of which may make a benevolent dictator look very attractive. There are no simple solutions, however, only a recognition that shared governance is an ongoing process always being redefined.

STAFF: SYMPATHETIC AND SKILLED

Teachers, realistic, flexible, idealistic, sensitive, creative, enthusiastic, facilitative, and skilled, are a sine qua non for our schools. The Eight-Year Study points out that their experience has shown that these paragons, in order to make the constant changes required of a flexible, student-oriented curriculum, require also "a sure sense of security in adventure" (Aikin 1942, 130).

Since the "teacher" role is shared by many, it might be useful to survey the major tasks that must be carried out if a school is to survive, and to explore different ways in which they might be accomplished.

The contractual agreements of public school teachers often limit their role playing flexibility, although the open school teachers often ignore their imposed legal limits because the needs and interests of their students defy compartmentalization.

The most important student need is the presence of an understanding, sensitive, friendly, enthusiastic, supportive, flexible, honest adult. This person provides a safe homebase for the young child and a knowledgeable companion, role model, and advisor for the older student. This person spends a great deal of time with the students and is available when needed. Most frequently this person is a paid, full-time staff member, whose presence is a solid, dependable fact.

In some aspects this teacher role can be likened to that of a surrogate parent. These schools may be similar to extended families, with important differences. While as compassionate and concerned as a parent, the open school teacher possesses professional expertise and objectivity. This teacher understands human development and is knowledgeable about the many ways in which humans learn. This full-time staff member doesn't need deep knowledge of narrow subject matter areas, but, whatever his or her interests and skills, must be filled with enthusiasm for living and learning and problem solving. This enthusiasm is tempered by self-knowledge, awareness of personal limits, the skill to recognize a student's need for expert knowledge, and a willingness to take risks and change.

At Upland Hills, the staff approaches filling a vacancy by looking for a candidate whose skills complement those of the rest of the staff. Then they report that they usually end up with someone quite different from their original ideal. Teachers in our schools are hired first on the basis of their personal qualities.

If student interest is high and staff subject matter expertise is weak, there are many sources of experts. Bob, a student, had spent two years at Natural Bridge sliding through the days with no particular enthusiasm or interests, until a gray gloomy morning when he announced he had made a decision. He had decided he wanted, even needed to learn the skills of drafting. The staff assessed their ability to meet Bob's driving desire to learn, and came up with a weak offer of a textbook and a little help. A trip through the Yellow Pages failed to uncover a willing expert draftsman. Finding resources requires patience and ingenuity, and employing some of both, the staff hit the jackpot. Bob could take a com-puter-based drafting course for architecture students in a local university. Of course, he would be restricted to those hours the college students left a computer free, but he eagerly followed up on these arrangements and even continued the course during his school vacations.

A most important task to be carried out in these schools is finding resources—people, places, and things—to meet the students' interests and needs. An "educational scavenger" and a "skills resource person" would be invaluable assets. A staff member in a small school might assume one or both of these responsibilities. Or parents or volunteers or committees could take on the tasks. No matter how the work is done, there must be excellent interpersonal communication among all involved.

In fact, it is this constant communication and planning that keeps a school going. Everyone—students, staff, volunteers, parents—becomes a team member. Teachers accustomed to running independent class-rooms as their own private kingdoms must adjust to survive.

No matter what their size, every open-ended school must have someone to look after the bookkeeping, publicity, and secretarial tasks. Finding transportation for the frequent travels and field trips is a constant need. Somebody has to attend to dull administrative details, to deal with inspectors and officials, to make sure necessary forms are completed on time, etc.

Then there are the problems of tuition collection (a private school nightmare), bill paying, and fundraising as well as building maintenance and maintaining necessary supplies. With local printing companies donating their odd-sized paper off-cuts, pencils, chalk, paper towels, toilet paper, and cat food were the most necessary supplies to purchase at one private school.

The problem of maintaining positive community relations bears special attention. Achieving legitimacy in the community is a long term task. The public, including parents, must be informed about school activities and achievements, interests, and needs. Detroit Open School sends parents a packet of informative news each Wednesday. If a packet fails to arrive by "kid mail," the parent immediately contacts the school. This school's success is fueled by good communication.

When students travel about and work in the community, they act as their own ambassadors. Students at Natural Bridge both contributed their art works to a university television station's fundraising auction, and worked as volunteers to make the auction a success. A Clonlara student organized his fellow students to broadcast weekly ten minute informative programs on a radio talk show. The Community High jazz band is recognized both locally and in Europe. In 1990 the band will perform concerts in Moscow and Leningrad.

Mention must again be made of evaluation. One aspect of evaluation is providing student feedback. Daily school activities may be so numerous and varied that everyone is off and running in a new direction before the results of the old have been analyzed. Yet we all may learn most when we sit back and evaluate our own work and compare our evaluations with those of others. At home each night, teacher Doris Sperling adds her own assessments to the student kept records. Meaningful student evaluation is accompanied by meaningful teacher evaluation.

Finally, program evaluation is most important, always being tied to the school's philosophy and goals. What is working? How can it be improved? What must be changed? What is being overlooked?

That last question touches reality. Without a person responsible for overseeing the many details which keep any school functioning, especially a nontraditional open school, someone, somehow, must take on the task of administration. This person does not necessarily have a great deal more authority, only a bit more responsibility. In a public program, the administrator becomes a most necessary advocate, defending the program's integrity from marauding forces. A very small private preschool might have no more administrative needs than could be met by an individual parent or by a small committee.

In these schools, students, parents, paid staff members, paid part-time teachers, and volunteers make up the staff.Each school works out its own facilitative pattern.

Separate Building and Facilities

"What do you think the Open Classroom Program and MYA need most to succeed?" the three building principals housing these programs were asked individually. Unanimously they said a separate building. Yet for a time these same principals had not allowed these teachers even to use adjacent rooms.

The kind of physical, emotional, and mental freedom these schools strive for may best be achieved when students, parents, and staff don't have to worry about disturbing others. Whether they are traditional teachers or students or community members, unhappy neighbors may try to bring grief to these schools. One such neighbor persisted in complaining to City Hall about Natural Bridge. Fortunately the officials were unable to find grounds for her criticisms and after many visits eventually became school friends. A school's separatism must be balanced by its goals. If a goal of the school is that students learn to be responsible members of their community, then that is where the school should be.

A nontraditional open school does not require a building with a large wall-free interior space. What is needed is freedom of movement in whatever spaces are available. At least one impoverished school (in a benign climate) used a public park as an educational setting (Graubard 1972).

Individual needs are respected in these schools, and physical arrangements should include space for noisy, active children as well as quiet-seeking children. The use of space is a question deeply interesting to most children and a problem to be discussed and decided by everyone together.

As Region Four Open School shows, innovative programs can coexist with traditional ones.

The halls are for learning at Detroit Open School. Photograph by Alex Korn.

Philosophy and Goals

The need for a positive philosophy and goals bears repeating. No institution can exist on a foundation of what it will not be.

Ideally the construction of a philosophy and educational goals is accomplished by everyone with a stake in the outcome working together. Why should their school exist? What are its purposes? What is their perception of the nature of humankind? What kind of people do they want their students and teachers to become? What qualities and skills should they possess? Discussions about these and other questions could go on forever without the participants reaching consensual conclusion. These discussions are bound to touch deep and conflicting emotions.

The philosophical swamps have trapped many unwary planners. Some have retreated in disgust while others cheerfully and blindly avoided the dangerous terrain. "We can't agree on a philosophy so let's just start a school," these optimists might have said. Blessed with extraordinary luck and a homogeneous group of parents and students, these optimists might survive a while, but a dissenter is bound to appear on the scene, ask all the unanswered questions, and try to reshape the school.

Moreover, teachers are bound to approach their work differently, and without a foundation for support and direction there is no way to assess the effectiveness of their different approaches. When the school is having problems, there is no place to turn to seek resolutions.

Frequently those interested in alternative education are so mistrustful of the inventions of others that they constantly try to reinvent the wheel. Yet existing models may be adapted to fit specific needs and desires. Detroit Open School was given a model of British informal education; it is a model to which the school director was knowledgeably committed. Parent discussion groups and teacher in-service training help others understand and implement that model. Pat Montgomery found inspiration in A.S. Neill's philosophy, but Clonlara only remotely resembles Summerhill; time, experience, culture, and personalities have recut the pattern to a different shape.

The design of a philosophical base starts with children and their reality. Johnny has not, will not, learn the alphabet. Does this make a difference? Mary only wants to play in the sand; what can she be learning? A philosophical approach may be distilled by understanding three-dimensional people.

The earliest philosophy statement of Upland Hills Farm School was created by a group, but the group left at the end of the first year. Many years later, new goals continue to evolve.

The Natural Bridge staff knew children have innate curiosity and possess an adaptive drive to understand and make sense of their world. While young people are perceptive and trustworthy, they lack the experience of adults. Thus the school functioned in a shifting, middle area, the staff assuming responsibility for turning over responsibility to the students. An unexpected exciting challenge turned out to be surviving the parent meetings where conflicting forces heatedly argued their opposing views: the school is too rigid/no this school is too free!

A school or program that retains the children only a few years runs special risks without a philosophical foundation. For most of its existence, MYA was only a two year program. (In 1989 the school district shifted from grade seven through nine intermediate schools to grade six through eight middle schools; MYA now is a three-year program.) Parents and teachers were involved in the initial planning, but the teaching staff has turned over many times. When a few parents with large families and long memories insist that the foundation and spirit of MYA are being violated, the current teachers are offended. They feel that MYA is what they are doing. There is neither time nor energy to re-create a mutually understood philosophy every two years.

There is truth in the MYA teachers' perception that the people in the school are the school. Thus, if the people in the school change drastically, the philosophy is in danger of losing its fit. Either the philosophy may have to be altered or the people changed. Evaluation of program effectiveness begins with its foundations. Perhaps they need modification. More often, day to day events within the school have moved the program farther and farther from its base. Always there is a tendency to drift towards a traditional mode.

UNDERSTANDING LAWS AND REGULATIONS

At some level all schools will have to deal with building inspectors, public health officials, insurance, fire inspectors, education officials, etc.

Enthusiastic idealists seldom like to handle details, and ignorance of important regulations has lead more than one school to fail even before opening. Such frustrations are to be avoided, if possible; there will be many others to take their place.

Certain techniques may be useful in dealing with officials. Letting a fire inspector find small, easily remedied violations may keep this official from ordering expensive technical alterations. Inspectors feel they are doing their jobs only when they find problems in need of remedy. Asking help and assistance from officialdom also may help bureaucrats learn that open school people are not strange aliens, but concerned humans.

It is particularly helpful to seek advice from authorities before making changes in a building. Asking a health inspector to talk with the students about the substance and reasons behind the regulations may produce twofold benefits: the inspector feels needed, and the students and staff may gain valuable information about their school environment and health. Smiling agreement with officialdom followed by indefinite foot-dragging delay in compliance also may be useful.

These are some realities of school existence. The dream is so different!

FUNDING

The public open classroom teachers would like to have control over some portion of the money allocated for their students. Teachers frequently spend their own salaries for small items invaluable to learning.

People attempting to start private schools must decide for themselves just how they will deal with their money problems, for problems there will be. Our three private schools have taken different approaches to paying their way. Yet they are united in being nonprofit institutions. Most of these schools not only are nonprofit, but also money-losing institutions.

Most of their money goes to people, not materials and buildings, although salaries frequently are much lower than those offered by public schools. There must be more than monetary rewards to working in these schools.

Pat and Jim Montgomery started Clonlara with borrowed money, and, although Pat has never drawn a salary, the student tuition fees have never covered expenses. As the expense of borrowing money soared, so did the school's deficit. For more than twenty years the school has performed a miraculous juggling act, an achievement which is likely to continue.

Fundraising is a chore most open schoolers not only deplore, but do poorly. Finding someone committed to the school's goals who actually likes to raise money might be the most important first step in school planning. Teachers often are required to join in fundraising activities, to scare up some of the cash to pay their own salaries, but this is a dreadful imposition on their time, energy, and preferences. Much better would be to find professionals with a basic interest in the school's survival. If possible.

Tuition fees at Natural Bridge rose with the school's credibility but never equalled the expenses; around 85 percent of tuition went to salaries. The reasons for this gap between income and outgo were many, including the cold, hard fact that some people may default on tuition payments, while the insurance man and the electrical company never stopped sending their bills, and too, the teachers always had to eat and pay their rent.

From time to time the staff daydreamed about being an affluent, carefree school, but in the end they decided that poverty was itself an education for the students. The students initiated ideas for and participated in fundraising. They learned to appreciate the value of the school's resources. When the students claimed they were fed up with having to clean their own school—"We pay to come here and we have to work, but in public school we never had to do any cleaning"—they phoned professional cleaning services and got astronomical estimates. So the reluctant cleaners decided they'd rather have their teachers than a professional cleaning service.

Upland Hills Farm School is able to balance its books from tuition payments alone. They are fortunate in having a long term, token payment lease on their land, and the staff and parents all have worked together to create their energy efficient buildings. As a result, almost all their income goes to the teachers who themselves perform the diverse duties listed in the previous section. Tuition payments may be decreased for parents able to provide services for which the school otherwise would have to pay.

Ideally the apportionment of school money is an issue which can be worked on by everyone. The reality is that financial decisions usually are made on the wing, after balancing many conflicting forces with the momentary availability of cash. The financial status of an open school may be so precarious that the young students would be unduly upset by participating in money decisions. Instead they might be given power to control the disbursement of small amounts of cash in mutually agreed upon ways.

Without a clear idea of their school's financial condition and participation in monetary decisions, staff members tend to harbor grudges toward those they feel control the money supply. The need to work and plan together cannot be overemphasized.

STUDENTS AND PARENTS

Obviously schools must have students and students must have parents. If no one is interested in a well-funded, ideally staffed, beautifully housed dream school based on a dazzling philosophy, it cannot become reality.

To exist, school programs must appeal to people, but the people first must have some knowledge of the programs on which to base their decisions. Education of the public is required both to start and to maintain a school. With a new school administration, Community High and MYA students and teachers at last are permitted to make recruiting presentations in elementary and intermediate schools, but some counselors have been hostile toward these programs of choice. Building good public relations with accurate information requires more time and energy than most alternative, open school people possess.

Enthusiasm stays high where a sense of belonging and active participation is nurtured. The amount of parent participation depends not only on the school goals and philosophy, but also on the realities of the parents' lives. In one community, a cooperative school might work beautifully because everyone has the necessary time to work together. In another most parents may be so busy that they have little time to spend in school decision making—at least not while the school is running well and to their liking.

A school which begins to lose students must re-examine and re-evaluate its purposes and performance. Our schools are schools of choice, and if students and teachers would prefer being elsewhere the school is under warning.

Networking

The people dreaming plans for a public open school on that stormy night in 1980 listed teacher in-service training as a requirement for success. They knew that all teachers, and especially open school teachers, need support and knowledge from others. This sharing and mutual support has increased slowly over the years of the Open Classroom Program and Bach Open School, but in its first years the teachers were especially isolated from one another. While they often wondered what their fellow teachers were up to, they lacked the time, energy, and mechanisms to get together; the pressing demands of the present always prevailed.

This is a school reality. The problems of dealing with each day are totally absorbing. There is little time to sit back and reflect. There is even less time and energy to link up with other schools with common goals.

Open schoolers sometimes are surprised to discover that they are not alone in the world. They need ways to connect with and learn from one another to keep abreast of developments. Networks of communication begin to provide this linking. Small local coalitions may lead to such very practical matters as sharing free materials—the school with a huge supply of carpet squares trades with the school with a ton of only slightly used paper. Or they may provide perspective and support, thereby strengthening the resolve and convictions damaged by day to day combat.

Through its newsletters and annual conferences, the members of the National Coalition of Alternative Community Schools learn of the activities of their fellows and encourage one another. Open schoolers tend to be independent-minded individualists, but they are strengthened by coming together.

In this chapter, ideals for survival have been identified in a number of areas. Each may be tempered by reality.

1. Ideally schools are staffed by compassionate, understanding, committed, flexible, creative, mature, developing, enthusiastic, talented, cooperative individuals. In reality, the staff members are imperfect humans who strive toward these qualities.
2. Ideally schools would have their own building or space, within which all school participants could exercise their freedom. Yet schools may grow and flourish almost anywhere, even without a building.
3. Ideally schools are maintained by reliable funding, the expenditure over which the schools, the staff, students, and parents, have significant control. In truth schools, particularly private schools, constantly must struggle and compromise their financial ideals.
4. Ideally schools both understand and comply with all relevant laws and regulations. Actually such conformity could mean the school could not become reality.
5. Community education and good public relations attract students and supporters to these schools.
6. Teachers must be able to share their questions and their successes and failures with one another. Similarly, participation in an active network of like-minded schools strengthens the individual school as ideas, skills, concepts, and materials are developed and shared.

Chapter 10

AFTERWORDS

Since the 1984 publication of the Japanese version of this book, *Free Schools: Reality and Dream*, American education, as a whole, has become more conservative, more, in fact, Japanese. Standardized testing has increased both in frequency and in importance. Television advertisements are claiming that a computer based program has propelled kindergartners to read *two years above grade level*! The program itself is interesting and certainly not unlike the paper and pencil techniques used in many open classrooms in which writing and reading are considered a natural extension of speaking. The problem is the expectation that kindergartners, five-year-olds, should be reading and reading well. The numbers of non-reading five-year-old failures are sure to swell.

Requirements for high school graduation are stiffer and more rigid. High expectations for the achievement of all students is something our innovative schools applaud, but the rigidity is foreign—and, they probably would observe, an effort doomed to fail.

At our President's 1989 "education summit," attended by the nation's governors and selected educators, everyone agreed that our schools are in trouble. As a result, a committee of governors and White House staff members is meeting to define national goals for education. An influential education critic advocates a "nationwide, grade-by-grade curriculum" in our elementary schools (*New York Times*, December 6, 1989). Exactly how these actions would relate to the "schools of choice" also promoted by the Bush Administration is confusing, to say the least.

While state-wide multiple choice competency tests are being developed to determine who should be allowed to graduate, while teachers are being subjected to their own multiple choice tests to determine who is eligible to teach, alternative schools have been flourishing.

In September of 1989, many school districts in British Columbia substituted an ungraded primary grouping for for their former kindergartens and grades one through three. Officials in the education ministry hope to see the province's dropout rate of nearly a third decrease as primary children are allowed to learn at their own rate with individualized instruction and are spared both graded report cards and grades on tests (*Denver Post*, May 28, 1989).

Ann Arbor's most recent school superintendent, Richard Benjamin, has supported the Open Classroom Program. After a year of planning (during which I held the position of open classroom coordinator) the OCP moved into its own building in September 1986 with its own principal selected by a committee of twenty-one, including administrators, teachers, parents, and students. Dr. Benjamin's support of open education is based on what he sees as its results. He says his observations and reading have convinced him that students partaking in open education become self-disciplined and self-motivated while they learn "higher order problem solving skills." He would like to identify the methodologies which makes these wonders occur and to utilize them in all schools. At the same time he advocates the "effective schools" approach which includes frequent standardized achievement testing for all students—a dilemma for the new 370 student kindergarten through sixth grade Bach Open School.

After years of firmly closing their classroom doors or constantly watching over their shoulders for enemies, these open school teachers are beginning to relax. There are new grade combinations; one teacher has students in grades one through four, and Joan Goldsmith includes kindergartners with her first, second, and third graders. Inevitably problems surface as these teachers learn to work together as a school instead of a group of individual classrooms, but the possibilities are real.

In Bach Open School's first year some parents, the principal, and a number of teachers remained at odds with one another. Their lack of shared trust effectively sabotaged many cooperative activities, and in the second year a new principal took over. Whatever its specific causes, this first year chaos was not surprising. The open, informal, classroom teachers had to be strong to survive year after year. The aggressive, activist parents had to be persistent and brilliant tacticians to keep the program they wanted alive. In its third year as a school, the program is not "perfect," but perfection is difficult to define. The effective operation of a form of shared governance requires constant effort. After many years of parental supremacy, a balance of decision making power is yet to be achieved. A teacher, for example, reported that two of her students, a first and a second grader, argued heatedly over whose mother actually was running the school while other children either looked on bewildered or argued that their parents, too, helped the school.

Middle Years Alternative remains housed in a traditional middle school, but for the first time has a waiting list. Now that the school district has turned its intermediate grade seven through nine schools into grade six through eight middle schools, MYA is one of three houses and has 134 students, six teachers, and an inhouse administrator, all of whom are learning to work together. The MYA classes consist of two hour blocks of combined subjects, either math and science or language arts and social studies. Because of scheduling difficulties some classes are single graded while others include sixth, seventh, and eighth graders.

Most of Community High School's 325 students continue to look absolutely outrageous, although one veteran teacher observes they seem "less activist" than in years past. Then she adds, "That's only until you go into another school. Then our students are the activists."

Throughout a traumatic year in which small, under-enrolled schools were fingered for closing and efforts were made to bring racial balance to all schools, Community High achieved an unfamiliar legitimacy with the school board and central administration. Naturally there was talk of selling the old elementary school in which the high school is housed. The neighborhood is turning upscale and the school's property value has soared; Community once again has had to descend on the school board to protect its turf. And once again the embattled high school was spared and has been given assurances that it is needed and has a right to exist.

Ann Arbor's high school curriculum has been tightened; twenty-two credits now are required for graduation and the choices of students in the traditional high schools are being curtailed. However, Community students and staff again have been told that they can continue to earn and grant credits in their flexible, creative ways, including individualized community resource contracts (around twenty-five traditional students have their own community resource contracts which will be honored by their home schools).

On the conservative side, fewer students are making use of community resources; with staff changes, the founding philosophy is collectively weakened. Few students even may be aware of their option to try experimental courses on a pass/fail basis.

Community High will be challenged soon by students and parents from the Bach Open School. Since the Open Classroom Program, Middle Years Alternative and Community were founded at different times, for different reasons, in their prior forms these programs led separate lives. Surprisingly, few former open classroom students enrolled in Community.

The importance of networking has been mentioned. During the year of planning the Bach Open School, teachers, parents, and elementary age students visited their counterpart in Detroit, and the Open Classroom Program in turn hosted a Detroit contingent. Although the home communities and student populations differ, as do their programs, the two schools share many common goals and problems.

As already has been seen, the former Region Four Open School has made great strides. Now it is the sole occupant of its building which has been renamed the Detroit Open School with Laurajean Milligan its acknowledged administrator. Hanging plants, colorful artwork, and children fill the corridors. Parents have raised money to buy more than twenty heavily used computers grouped together in the former social studies classroom. The middle school is functioning more smoothly; in one grade six-seven class, boys and girls, black and white, are gathered in a comfortable, self-selected mix around large, round tables—a remarkable sight compared with the cliquish seating by sex, race, and social status in most junior high schools. The Detroit Open School pattern of CAT scores has not changed, and the staff continues largely to ignore their standardized achievement test results. More than six hundred persistent people remain on the waiting list.

Upland Hills Farm School is on an emotional high. On a Rotary International Foundation exchange trip to India, Phil Moore visited a half dozen countries, including Japan where he gave a talk to members of the Free School Study Association. With new ideas and new energy, the staff seems both more cohesive and excited. "We no longer only are surviving year by year," Phil says. "We're trying to put in place a new educational scenario for spaceship earth. At first all we wanted was to provide loving care, a place where children wouldn't be damaged, and we did that. Now we want Leonardos, kids who become excited about learning and inquiry. We want our students to become agents of change, to be the Nobel prize winners, to leave school secure in the knowledge that they have the gift to make people laugh, to be a scientist or a statesman."

At Upland Hills the morning work now is structured around developmentally appropriate comprehensive units, for example, grandparents or weather. The older students participate in a thinking program based on Cognitive Research Trust Court Lessons. All students are encouraged to participate both actively and in depth in the variety of afternoon choice classes—the Renaissance Leonardo has a multitude of interests and skills.

Parent enthusiasm has spearheaded efforts to raise money to construct a real school building with foundations and thoughtful planning to replace the two aged portable classrooms and student-built geodesic dome on a hilltop; construction is underway.

Perhaps the greatest changes have taken place at Clonlara, less in daily school life than in organizational emphasis. Offices and desks have replaced preschoolers. Pat Montgomery says that she and her staff are supervising homeschooling for about twelve hundred students. The thirty-four on-campus students include first graders and high school seniors. Three brothers and their mother have come to Clonlara from Sapporo, Japan; they add both diversity and instruction. Many students are gaining proficiency in Japanese as the Japanese students learn English. The two full-time teachers are experienced and enthusiastic. During lunchtime on a gray, snowy day the younger children are busy with everything from a science experiment to writing and painting, to block building. From time to time they pause to nibble on their sandwiches. The portable classrooms have been refurbished and reorganized; maximum tuition has increased significantly, although students still pay on a sliding scale.

These days Pat Montgomery is most likely to be found lobbying in Lansing or in attorneys' offices and courtrooms.

The changes in our schools through 1988 are summarized in Chart 6.

Clonlara's home schooling program extends to Japan where school phobia is a pervasive childhood disorder. In the monthly Free School Study Group's newsletter, parents and teachers share their experiences. The organization has around seven hundred members, one hundred fifty of them new this year. In the newsletter, a mother deplored an educational system which identifies school phobic children and their families as a problem requiring treatment instead of changing the way in which the schools are operated. (In Japan many children who are deeply afraid of going to school are hospitalized for treatment.) Japanese children taught at home are ineligible for the junior high school diplomas which are required to qualify for college entrance tests; so far this remains an insoluble problem, although one parent suggested she might pay to enroll her child in a private school, while he actually stays home.

CHART 6
How They Changed

Schools	Enrollment 1983	1988	Changes Other Significant Changes
Clonlara	55	34	Preschool eliminated. Large home schooling program.
OCP/Bach Open School	256	370	Has own building. Has own principal and selected support staff. Kindergarten added. Classroom teachers added. New age groupings, etc.
MYA	94	85	Has wing of building. Teachers working together. Two house block of time for MYA classes.
Region Four/ Detroit Open School	415	415	Has own building. Computer room equipped by parents. Professional librarian. Selected support staff.
Upland Hills	52	47	New school building funded by parents. Enriched and expanded curriculum.
Community High	293	325	New dean. Administrative assurance of viability.

Creativity remains a rare attribute in Japan and its scarcity is said to be hobbling that nation's software development among other creative endeavors. "Computer giants here," reports the Sunday, December 7th, 1986 *New York Times*, "are breaking tradition and bidding top dollar for the best software talent they can find, often importing it from the United States." On December 8th another newspaper printed a portrait of solemn Japanese business men, faces coated with cosmetic facial masks, engaged in a seminar on "originality and persuasion." Successful products of a uniform educational system probably will be changed little by uniformly applied cosmetics.

Back in the United States both uniformity and diversity have their advocates. A recognition of the need for diversity is underway in Detroit where the public school system recently established an Office of City-Wide Alternative Schools and Programs to help coordinate the city's numerous and philosophically diverse magnet schools. The superintendent appointed a parental choice task force to study the "Schools of Choice within the district and throughout the United States to make recommendations to maintain and improve educational offerings to students" (Detroit Public Schools, 1987, p. 2). Partly because of the earlier decentralization efforts, partly because of the different origins of these schools—everything from court order to parental pressure—this was the first time those involved in the alternative schools and programs had got together. Outside experts and consultants, including Mary Anne Raywid, have come from St. Paul, St. Louis, Cambridge, and New York City to share insights and experiences.

With academic diversity, administrators hope to draw more students back to city schools, to provide greater choice to ambivalent parents and turned off students, to increase morale, and to boost the learning of at-risk students. Academic diversity recognizes that not all children learn in exactly the same manner—although all can learn. Research in environmental design (Barker and Wright 1951; Krasner 1980) confirms that an environment itself may elicit certain behaviors.

Raywid argues that an environmental design approach to education "presupposes that there is no one best way to keep school, no one best curriculum in the sky, no one best way to teach reading or anything else, no one best way to test for or measure education accomplishment" (1985, 5); and thus we return to our innovative schools and their appreciation of the importance of respecting and understanding the whole individual student.

Experience has demonstrated that it is possible to develop educational environments responsive to students and the totality of their talents, needs, skills. Research has recorded their short and long term effectiveness.

Our idealistic alternative schools can provide models and nourishing food for thought to both American and Japanese educational planners. A veteran educational researcher whose evaluations of educational reforms date back to the Eight-Year Study would add time as another necessary ingredient for school change. "In my work on school improvement," Ralph Tyler wrote recently, "I have found that it takes six or seven years to get a reform really working as intended. Most implementation plans greatly underestimate the amount of time required" (Tyler 1987, 280).

Our tendency in America is to look for quick fixes. Our traditional educational designs may be likened to imperfectly realized factory production lines. If the products of the assembly line are flawed, if they cannot read, or think creatively, or compute, then, we reason, the assembly line processes must be changed. Perhaps an adjustment is needed in textbooks or worksheets or tests.

Deficient automobiles are not held responsible for their short circuits and mechanical failures, but humans are. We both are created by and held accountable to our society. Our skills, our sense of self worth, even our values (for we learn from experience) are developed in our schools. Our schools must shoulder their share of responsibility.

A highly competitive school technology which turns out a few superior products while also producing many functional and even nonfunctional illiterates is doubly ineffective. Of course the destruction of human potential is expensive both to individuals and to society. But the successful products of a rigid, narrow educational system also may harm society, as the Japanese search for creativity reminds us.

Our assembly lines now are being serviced by man-made robots instead of trained humans, and our fundamental human problems are growing more complex. We will continue to need citizens who have the skills to read, write, and even compute, or at least the ability to make estimates in order to catch calculator/computer malfunctions. But an even greater need for the survival of our democratic society is a thinking, problem-solving citizenry. The findings of the Eight-Year Study may be important to our future. The attributes in which those experimental students excelled could be a good starting place; what's wrong with greater than usual enthusiasm for learning, intellectual curiosity and drive, resourcefulness, precision and objectivity in thinking, awareness of world happenings, creativity, cooperation, and independence?

Our innovative schools stress the worth and potentials of all people, including parents and teachers whoever they may be. These educational environments are future oriented while totally involved in an all-encompassing present. In these schools education begins with people, not with systems.

They should not be ignored.

Appendix

SCHOOL MODELS

These innovative schools were created to serve real people in actual locations. Each is an original model but not entirely dissimilar from other organizational models. In this appendix, a number of models are presented with their basic requirements, advantages, and disadvantages. The models are not mutually exclusive; most are permutations and combinations of basic building blocks.

Dissatisfaction with the status quo is a starting point for all. Parents fear their children will not attain what they have dreamed for them. Some perceive a growing gap between societal transformations and the realities and goals of traditional education. Some fear that educational institutions conspire to eradicate valuable human qualities.

Children may become hostile and disruptive at home or refuse to go to school. Young children may change from eager learners to unhappy students. The stress of being "educated" leads some young people to self-defeating, even self-destructive, behaviors.

Caught between the external demands of their jobs and the needs of their students, teachers are frustrated by externally imposed curricula.

When such people get together, their ideals take on various organizational forms.

COOPERATIVE SCHOOL

Cooperative schools may be created by a group of congenial dreamers, usually parents, who decide they possess both the desire and the skills necessary to run their own school. All participants have the right and responsibility to share in all decisions. While a formally educated teacher may be part of the group, much of the work will be carried out cooperatively by participating parents.

This type of school often is small and the children young.

Advantages. Cooperative schools usually are inexpensive to establish. Because everyone participates in decisions and shares the work, there is a strong sense of ownership.

This school is a normal extension of a young child's homelife. The child's circle of friends expands naturally. Concerned parents always are present and the child is not abandoned to an unfamiliar social world. Parents may be very perceptive to the children's needs because they are attuned immediately and practically to every child's present stage of development.

Parents work together as a group. The potential for growth and development exists not only for the children, but also for their parents.

As new parents and children join in a cooperative, the philosophy and goals constantly are being scrutinized. Cooperative decision making is available as a corrective process to help find solutions to the inevitable problems.

Disadvantages. Decisions require time and patience. Because the school depends on the cooperation of all, it lacks the flexibility to change plans rapidly.

The program may be based on the skills of the participating parents and as the parents change, so does the program. It may be difficult to maintain program stability. (This disadvantage may well be seen as an advantage by some, for a cooperative school always is changing, resisting the pressures towards rigidity and ossification.)

As their children grow and become more independent, parents may become less interested in being actively involved in their school and necessary tasks may not be completed. Attendance at decision-making meetings may fall off drastically. While the school will be a cooperative in name, the persistent, hardworking minority will be making the decisions. The hardworking members may feel used by the others, who, in turn, may be suspicious of the motives and quality of the hard workers' decisions.

Over time, the school is rebuilt by the decisions of those participating; it may change radically and be unrecognizable to its founders. This factor may be seen as a plus or a minus.

INDIVIDUAL FOUNDERS

A single individual may develop an educational philosophy and attract interested followers. As others join in, the authority and power of the founder probably are shared. The individual founder, however, may remain the person of last resort, the one who bears ultimate responsibility for the school's continuation.

Fewer educational compromises may be necessary in this school model than any other. Its longevity is dependent on the founder's attracting others who believe so deeply in the school's premises that they will put as much effort into the school's continuation as the founder.

Because these usually are private schools, funding is a continuous problem aggravated by the truth that most people attracted to these innovative schools abhor fundraising. Financing the beginning of the school usually is the founder's heavy burden.

Often a board of directors of parents, community members, influential community leaders, professional educators, participate in guiding the school. A committed board of directors is particularly invaluable to a school started by an individual.

Clonlara was founded by an individual. If, for some reason, Pat Montgomery had to leave, the school probably would cease to exist. Natural Bridge School dissolved two years after I left as a daily physical presence.

Advantages. A single school founder is able to make decisions rapidly to put his or her personal educational philosophy and goals in practice. Fewer compromises must be made than in most models of school organization.

Because the ultimate responsibility for continuation of the school may rest on one individual, that person is dedicated and identifiable. The school founder is synonymous with the school and works singlemindedly in the school's behalf.

Disadvantages. Funding and other school-starting responsibilities are not shared. The school will fail if the founder must leave without having found a successor or an organization that would assure the school's survival.

If there are school problems, and they are inevitable, the single founder is pointed out as the identifiable culprit.

The school founder may be reluctant to share power with others and resist needed changes.

Sharing responsibility, power, and authority may be a time-consuming, difficult process.

GRADUAL MODIFICATION OF EXISTING SCHOOLS

Public or private, preschool or high school, all are able to change the status quo in small ways. Individuals or entire schools might make the effort to change their practices. PALS members hoped the presence of informal classrooms would permanently alter traditional educational procedures, and for that reason some advocates of open education resisted consolidation into a single building.

At some point revolutionaries who attempt gradual change in existing programs will find someone, often their worst enemy, peering critically down their throats. An individual teacher probably will be ordered to justify her or his actions. At this point the forward-looking teacher will produce personal documentation of the results of his or her deviations from dogma. How have the children responded? How do the students feel? Records may justify the teacher's actions.

If a group of teachers in a given school band together to bring about change, their group records should contain evidence of both student success and parental enthusiasm by which to educate confrontational educational authorities.

Advantages. Because these are small modifications in existing programs there are no start up costs or expenses. Changes can take place almost immediately; there may be little time lag between origination and execution of the ideas.

Disadvantages. Ultimately some disapproving authority will notice and ask for an accounting. Changes take place at a frustratingly slow pace and results may be barely discernable.

UNDERGROUND SCHOOLS

Some choose to evade authorities and establish invisible learning environments. For obvious reasons these tend to be small enterprises hiding in out-of-the-way locations. Perhaps two or three sets of parents simply decide to keep their children at home when they reach school age and work together to provide what they feel is a good education. Such arrangements are not costly in cash, but require energy and a watchful eye to make sure they are meeting their own goals and needs.

A school established outside regulations may have a long life. We know of one stimulated by A.S. Neill's thinking that has existed in this manner for at least twelve years. It is not listed in the phone book and in several moves to new locations has evaded all but the public health inspector. Supportive visitors are welcome, but first they must find the school.

Both parents and educational authorities will be concerned that the students are acquiring appropriate skills in underground schools. Of course the parents, students, and authorities may not agree on the nature of those skills.

Advantages. Putting underground schools into operation may be cheap and fast. Beyond the constraints of maintaining invisibility, they have almost unlimited flexibility.

Some have housed themselves in moving vehicles. A bus provides space for study and learning while constantly traveling to new learning environments.

Disadvantages. Almost inevitably authorities will catch up and the school will face whatever legal consequences the authorities can muster.

Low visibility may lead to isolation from those working for the same goals. It also means that some learning experiences are risky.

RESEARCH-BASED SCHOOL

The thirty experimental secondary schools of the Eight-Year Study rode a crest of interest in an educational movement. They became part of a well-designed experiment in which long accepted beliefs about the relationships between secondary and university education were tested. Most of the schools would not have been able to change themselves without the assurance that the universities would honor the experimental design and admit students educated in an unorthodox manner. Experimentation on such a large scale is most rare. But school planners may gain legitimacy and support by offering themselves as research subjects.

A university, a philanthropic foundation, or a governmental organization might be convinced that the dreamers' ideas are designed to meet needs overlooked by traditional schools. The school planners first would have to contact potential influential researchers and present a good case for the merits of their educational approach to those skeptical social scientists in power. To the extent that the dreamers' views of pressing educational problems overlap with those of the powerful they may be successful in gaining support.

While trying to build their own school they must be judicious in expressing negative opinions about traditional education. Just as a school philosophy should be positive, so should publicity and propaganda.

Advantages. By becoming part of a research study the new school or program gains instant access to many school survival needs. The problems of acquiring space, a staff, students, funds (until the research is completed) and gaining legitimacy could be vastly simplified.

Because any sensible study of educational outcomes should continue for many years, the school would be granted a degree of stability.

Disadvantages. The dreamers have the danger of losing control and ownership of what was their school idea. Their own children might be refused admission if they fail to meet the requirements of the experimental design.

Support may not be enough to make a go of the program. The experimental schools in the Eight-Year Study did not receive financial assistance, but a major contributor threatened at least one private school with loss of support because of its participation in the project.

The most significant results of open, innovative education are not easily documented. Deep understanding of this kind of education is necessary to design meaningful research.

The end of research might lead to the termination of the school.

Because researchers may study the wrong factors or may be unable to measure the most important outcomes, the school experiment might, in the end, be considered a failure by the test of research. The parents who have seen their children grow and flourish in the experimental school may be forced to repeat the process of school creation.

Other factors which affect the operation of different school models include:

SCHOOL HOUSING

The physical environment is a reality which may enhance or weaken a school. Designers of school buildings tend to take themselves very seriously. They like people to believe that a school's success or failure is an an outgrowth physical plant. Actually the details of the physical school environment may be the least important factor in its survival. People are first and foremost.

Open school people are ingenious in adapting space to their needs. The school in a park has been mentioned. The idea of a school in a train or subway station is intriguing. Some schools find space in churches. Often buildings previously used for public gatherings are subject to fewer zoning and building restrictions.

The school on wheels has been mentioned, but how about a school in a department store?

It has been suggested that school survival is aided by space and the freedom to use that space without reprisal or fear of reprisal, but two forms of shared space deserve special mention.

School Without Walls

The school without walls attempts to break down physical and educational barriers between young people and the community they live in. In simpler times a young apprentice experienced real world learning. As the world grew more complex, students have become increasingly isolated from the world around them. Ordinarily today's students not only must remain confined with age mates for twelve years but are grouped by CATs, MEAPs, and SATs.

Traditional school buildings may be irrelevant to schools without walls. The community and its places of business and institutions become the school. Founded in Philadelphia in 1968, Parkway, the original school without walls, is still functioning today. Community High is a less dramatic version of the school without walls.

Advantages. The possibilities for experiential learning are almost limitless. Students are able to engage in exciting, meaningful learning. Career education comes from experience, not textbooks.

Barriers between students and the community are broken. Adults may see adolescents as genuine people and vice versa. Because many community members are active participants, the school develops a broad base of support.

There is little or no expense for elaborate facilities.

Disadvantages. Organization is complex. Students may slip through organizational cracks. Record keeping is very important.

Although a fully equipped high school is not required, a home base for students and staff is necessary.

School Within a School

Much already has been said about sharing buildings with traditional programs. The Open Classroom Program and MYA suffered many of the disadvantages of shared buildings. Region Four Open School overpowered its traditional building mate. With declining elementary enrollment the open school students kept the traditional Burgess School open for neighborhood children.

Advantages. A school within a school allows for choice and diversity within a single institution. Students can select a program which best fits their interests and learning style.

Expensive facilities such as libraries and gymnasiums can be shared.

As members of a small unit students no longer are victims of impersonal mass education.

Disadvantages. The majority program may look down upon others as lesser members of the school community.

The staff has to balance responsibilities between the parent institution and their own smaller unit.

The smaller nontraditional programs do not have the freedom to pursue their own interests in their own way.

While appearing equal on budget sheets, the financial support of the nontraditional programs may be less. The budgetary allotments may be for textbooks or services the nontraditional program does not require.

AGES OF STUDENTS

All these school models may enroll students of all ages, but the pros and cons of starting schools for people of various ages and developmental levels merit separate consideration.

Add-On School

Clonlara is an example of an add-on school. It started with a handful of preschoolers and added grades as they aged. Both staff and students had

time to learn and grow at an easy pace. The shocks of startup were min-
imized.

This model may work best for young children. Growing by adding
grades may be more difficult for high school students. Natural Bridge,
for example, had anticipated adding high school grades as the middle
school youngsters aged, but soon had to recognize severe problems. Most
high school students should have a larger group of friends than the few
available at Natural Bridge. More important, they also needed expensive
facilities and supplies to be able to pursue their awakened interests, especially in science and music.

Advantages. The add-on school, particularly one beginning with
young children, can start easily and inexpensively.

Disadvantages. The school planners must be ever alert to meeting the
needs of older children. Sometimes it is easier to continue that which one
docs well, for example, to provide an excellent educational environment
for young children, than to change the school for older youth.

It is tempting to try to be all things to all people instead of concen-
trating in a particular area of excellence.

Fixed Age Range

School dreamers may have a clear idea of the ages and developmental
levels for which their school is designed. Community High School, the
Open Classroom Program, and Upland Hills Farm School began with a
full range of students.

Startup shock may be unavoidable in such schools. The students
and staff must make adjustments and be willing to expend time and energy in learning together how to become a school. Because so much energy
is unleashed at one time, the school quickly may develop exciting educational programs appropriate to the particular students.

Advantages. Excellent school programs may be developed rapidly,
geared to the developmental needs of the students.

The school has a fixed identity.

Regular expenses can be anticipated and planned for. The budget
process is more predictable.

Disadvantages. Startup shock is almost inevitable. The initial expenditure of money, time, and energy is great.

Once the program or school is functioning as smoothly as such schools ever may, the staff, having flourished with adversity and stress, may become bored! Staff dissatisfaction and turnover should be anticipated at this point.

Full Age Range

Only brief mention will be made of the exciting possibility of a school for students of all ages, from the very young baby in infant care to those old in years but young in spirit. Parents and grandparents might learn and teach along with children.

The details of such a school may be left to the dreamers, although it might start on a limited basis and gradually expand to a school in which children could learn history and customs from their elders and adults could learn computers and science from the youth, and babies could be cared for and cherished by all.

HOME SCHOOLING

Not so long ago, education for most began and ended in the home. After the turn of the century, with exceptions, most children were educated in schools. Everyone was expected to attend a school, whether public, a private religion based school, or a secular independent private school. Education had become an activity for the professionals.

Yet individuals have been confident they had something special to offer their children. One, Dr. Adolph Berle, Sr., developed a system of home schooling through which his children were spectacularly successful. Thomas Evans, a law student at Harvard under Dr. Berle's son, Adolph A. Berle, rediscovered these methods and adapted them in his own book, *The School in the Home* (1973).

For different reasons, today a growing number of people are choosing to bypass institutional schools and to educate their children at home. The exact number of those teaching their school age children at home is imprecise at best. Those who assist home schoolers estimate the true number lies somewhere between between 50,000 and 250,000 children. The number of home schoolers definitely has increased since the 1981 publication of John Holt's book, *Teach Your Own*. (The book also has been translated into Japanese.)

All but nine states recognize home schooling as an educational alternative, although the laws differ substantially from state to state.

Public school authorities do not take these defections lying down, and, sometimes in ignorance of their own laws, try to force parents to return their children to the traditional schools.

To help parents provide home schooling, Clonlara established a Home Based Education Program in 1979. It began with two families and in 1984 enrolled 264 families. Clonlara helps the parents set up and maintain a home school, provides a curriculum based on each state's standards, keeps records if necessary, provides information about materials, and evaluates the students with the California Achievement Test. Clonlara also takes on the responsibility of dealing with troublesome officials and other administrative problems the home schoolers may encounter.

All types of people are involved in home schooling; their diverse reasons do include disillusionment with the effectiveness of educational institutions, but a great number hold strong religious beliefs which they fear will be weakened by school attendance.

Parents, like Dr. Berle, may be successful in educating their children at home. Home schooling is, perhaps, the ultimate in free choice.

REFERENCES

Aikin, Wilford M. *The Story of the Eight-Year Study with Conclusions and Recommendations.* New York: Harper & Brothers, 1942.

Anderson, Ronald S. *Education in Japan: a Century of Modern Development.* Washington D.C.: U. S. Department of Health, Education, and Welfare, Office of Education. U.S. Government Printing Office, 1975.

Ann Arbor Public Schools. Department of Research and Evaluation. "The Relationship of Classroom Organizational Style to Student Achievement." Ann Arbor Public Schools, 1981.

Ann Arbor Public Schools. Department of Research and Evaluation. "An Assessment of the Progress toward Implementation of the Open Classroom Program at Wines and Pattengill Schools." Ann Arbor Public Schools, 1983.

Barker, Roger G., and Paul V. Cump. *Big School Small School: High School Size and Student Behavior.* Stanford: Stanford University Press, 1964.

Barker, Roger G., and Herbert Wright. *One Boy's Day.* New York: Harper & Brothers, 1951.

Barr, Robert D. "Alternatives for the Eighties: A Second Decade of Development." *Phi Delta Kappan*, April 1981, 570-573.

Berrueta-Clement, John R., Lawrence J. Schweinhart, W. Steven Barnett, Ann S. Epstein, and David P. Weikart, *Changed Lives: the Effects of the Perry Preschool Program on Youths through Age 19.* Ypsilanti: High/Scope Educational Research Foundation, 1984.

Carini, Patricia F. *The School Lives of Seven Children: a Five Year Study*. North Dakota Study Group on Evaluation, 1982.

Case, Barbara J. "Lasting Alternatives: a Lesson in Survival." *Phi Delta Kappan*, April 1981, 554-557.

Deal, Terrence E., and Robert R. Nolan. "An Overview of Alternative Schools." In *Alternative Schools*, Terrence E. Deal and Robert R. Nolan eds. 1-18. Chicago: Nelson-Hall, 1978.

Detroit Public Schools. *Schools of Choice: Unique Educational Alternatives 1986/1987*. Detroit Board of Education, 1986.

Dewey, John. "Traditional v. Progressive Education." In *Alternative Schools*, Terrence E. Deal and Robert R. Nolan eds. 21-29. Chicago: Nelson Hall, 1978.

Dewey, John, and Evelyn Dewey. *Schools of Tomorrow*. New York: E.P. Dutton & Co., Inc., 1962.

Duke, Daniel Linden. "Great (and Dissimilar) Expectations: The Growth of the Albany Area Open School." In *Alternative Schools*, Terrence E. Deal and Robert R. Nolan eds. 175-190. Chicago: Nelson-Hall, 1978.

Evans, Thomas W. *The School in the Home*. New York: Harper and Row, 1973.

Featherstone, Joseph. "The Primary School Revolution in Britain." *New Republic*, August 1967.

Fuller, R. Buckminster. *On Education*. Boston: University of Massachusetts Press, 1979.

Goodlad, John I. *A Place Called School*. New York: McGraw Hill Book Co., 1984.

Graubard, Allen. *Free the Children: Radical Reform and the Free School Movement*. New York: Pantheon Books, 1972.

Henly, Martin. "Something is Missing from the Educational Reform Movement." *Phi Delta Kappan*, December 1987, 284-285.

Holt, John. *What Will I Do on Monday?* New York: E.P. Dutton & Co., Inc., 1970.

——— . *Teach Your Own*. New York: Delacorte Press, 1982.

Hori, Shin-ichiro. "A.S. Neill and Education in Japan." Manuscript, Osaka City University, 1982.

Horwitz, R. A. "Psychological Effects of the 'Open Classroom.'" *Review of Educational Research* 49 (1979): 71-86.

Hunt, J. McV. *Intelligence and Experience*. New York: Ronald Press Co., 1961.

————. "Intrinsic Motivation and Its Role in Psychological Development." In *Nebraska Symposium on Motivation*, David Levine ed. 189-192. Lincoln: University of Nebraska Press, 1965.

Krasner, Miriam. "Environmental Design in the Classroom." In *Environmental Design and Human Behavior*, Leonard Krasner ed. 302-319. Elmsford, New York: Pergamon Press, 1980.

Krasner, Miriam, and Gerald L. Hanley. "On Evaluating Open Education." *Education*, 105 (1984):206-213.

Jennings, Wayne, and Joe Nathan. "Startling/Disturbing Research on School Program Effectiveness." *Kappan*, March 1977.

Kohl, Herbert. *Basic Skills*. Boston: Little, Brown and Co., Inc., 1982.

Kuroyanagi, Tetsuko. *Totto-Chan: the Little Girl at the Window*. Tokyo: Kodansha, 1981.

Lohr, Steve. "Japan's New Non-Conformists." *New York Times*, March 8, 1983.

————. "The Japanese Challenge; Can They Achieve Technological Supremacy?" *The New York Times Magazine*, July 8, 1984.

McCauley, Brian, and Sanford Dornbusch. "Students Who Choose Alternative Public High Schools—Their Background, Their Education and Their Achievement: A Comparison of Matched Samples." In *Alternative Schools*, Terrence E. Deal and Robert R. Nolan eds. 211-230. Chicago: Nelson-Hall, 1978.

Murphy, David. "Trauma and Renaissance: A Case History of an Alternative School's Evolution." In *Alternative Schools*, Terrence E. Deal and Robert R. Nolan eds. 136155. Chicago: Nelson-Hall, Chicago, 1978.

Nathan, Joe. *Free to Teach*. New York: The Pilgrim Press, 1983.

Neill, A.S. *Summerhill*. New York: Hart Publishing Co., 1960.

Neill, A.S. "The Idea of Summerhill." In *Alternative Schools*, Terrence E. Deal and Robert R. Nolan eds., 30-37. Chicago: Nelson-Hall, 1978.

Ohnuma, Yasushi. *Kyoiku-ni-kyosei-wa-iranai*. Tokyo: Ikkosha Publishing Co., 1981.

Raywid, Mary Anne. "The Alternative in Alternatives." Project on Alternative Education, Hofstra University, 1980.

————. "The First Decade of Public School Alternatives." *Phi Delta Kappan*, April 1981, 551-554.

————. "Schools of Choice: Their Current Nature and Prospects." *Phi Delta Kappan*, June 1983, 684-688.

————. "Preparing Teachers for Schools of Choice." Paper read at the National Commission on Excellence in Teacher Education, 4 October 1984, at Austin, Texas. Mimeographed.

————. "Keeping At-Risk Youth in School." *State Education Leader*, Spring 1985, 4-6.

Rohlen, Thomas P. *Japan's High Schools*. Berkeley: University of California Press, 1983.

Salmans, Sandra. "Child Care Wars." *New York Times Education Magazine*, Spring 1989, 39-40.

Smith, Eugene R., Ralph Tyler, et al. *Appraising and Recording Student Progress* New York: Harper & Brothers, 1942.

St. John, C., and D. Harman. *Adult Illiteracy in the U.S.*. New York: McGraw Hill, 1979.

Thompson, E. W., and H. Shein. "An evaluation of the Middle Years Alternative Program." Office of Research and Evaluation, Ann Arbor Public Schools, 1978.

Trager, James. *Letters from Sachiko*. London: Abacus, 1984.

Tyler, Ralph W., "Education Reforms." *Phi Delta Kappan*, December 1987, 277-280.

Wallach, Michael. "Psychology of Talent and Graduate Education." Paper presented at the International Conference on Cognitive Styles and Creativity in Higher Education, sponsored by the Graduate Record Examinations Board, Montreal 1972.

Weikart, D. P., A. S. Epstein, L. Schweinhart and J.T. Bond. *The Ypsilanti Preschool Curriculum Demonstration Project*. Ypsilanti: High/Scope Educational Research Foundation, 1978.

Willis, Margaret. *The Guinea Pigs after Twenty Years: A Follow-up Study of the Class of 1938 of the University School Ohio State*. Columbus: Ohio State University Press, 1961.

L

Learning disabilities, and alternative education, 65, 84
Literacy, 1

M

McPherson, Bruce, 45
Mead, Margaret, 40
Middle school alternative education, curriculum in, 57-61; philosophy of, 133; staffing of, 29-30; teacher planning in, 115-116; and volunteers, 128 . *See also* Middle Years Alternative; Natural Bridge School
Middle Years Alternative (Ann Arbor, Mich.), 75, 118; and achievement test results, 97-98; curriculum in, 58; description of, 26, 141; history of, 29-30; philosophy of 133; problems of, 30; teacher selection in, 69-70
Miextyn, Dan, 26
Milligan, Laurajean, 32-34, 58, 62-63, 105
Montessori, Maria, 3
Montgomery, Pat, 112, 132, 134; and Clonlara School, 36, 37, 149; and home schooling, 143; in Japan, 5
Moore, Phil, 40, 142
Mrs. Marrietta Johnson's Organic School (Fairhope, Ala.), 2

N

National Coalition of Alternative Community Schools, 22, 137
Natural Bridge School (Tallahassee, Fla.), 64, 74-75, 112, 113, 139; and achievement tests, 78; and achievement test results, 99; curriculum in, 52, 60-61, 63; description of, 41; funding of, 121, 135; history of, 41-43; and reactions to freedom, 116-117; philosophy of, 42, 133; and student outcomes, 107; and student selection, 107; and teacher selection, 69
Neill, Alexander S., 3, 4-5, 36, 37, 38, 86
Nolan, Robert R., 40

O

Ohio State University Laboratory School, 102-103
Ohnuma, Yasushi, 5
Open Classroom Program (Ann Arbor, Mich.), achievement test results in, 97; admission to, 29; curriculum in, 54-55; description of, 25-26; evaluation in, 80-81; expense of, 120; governance in, 126-127; history of, 28-29, 123-124, 136; and student outcomes, 107; support of, 140; and teacher/parent relationships, 29, 141; teacher selection in, 72
Open education, and achievement test outcomes, 97-98; in British Columbia, 140; and British informal education, 3; and classroom organization, 10, 12; compared with traditional education, 31; and curriculum,